THE WAY OF THE PROFIT

To those who are givers and wonder whether God cares about your desires and material wealth, I can attest he most certainly does.

To my loving wife Wanda, and our children, Megan, Corinne, Evan and our future grandchildren. I wrote this book for you guys. Embrace things that seem hard and don't run from them, pursue what seems impossible and live for God. In these, you will always find His immeasurable love, waiting to reward you with great treasures.

Website: http://www.LOUDpublishing.com
Email: info@loudpublishing.com

ISBN: 978-1-7379877-0-3 (paperback)
ISBN: 978-1-7379877-2-7 (hardback)
ISBN: 978-1-7379877-1-0 (ebook)

Ordering Information:
Special discounts are available on quantity purchases by corporations, associations, and others. For details, contact me at info@danieltezeno.com or go to http://www.danieltezeno.com.

CONTENTS

BUILDING MATERIAL WEALTH THROUGH YOUR SPIRITUAL SELF

THE WAY OF THE PROFIT

DANIEL TEZENO

SECTION I: THE WAY YOU'RE MADE

CHAPTER 1

JUST LIKE YOUR FATHER

"It is the heart that makes a man rich. He is rich or poor according to what he is, not according to what he has."

—*Henry Ward Beecher[1]*

My wife and I love to watch movies. One of my all-time favorites is the animated classic drama *The Lion King* by Walt Disney Pictures. This touching but tragic story is about a lion cub named Simba who is destined to one day become protector and king over the pride as successor to the current king, his father Mufasa, and queen, his mother Sarabi. The story opens with a fantastic, uplifting musical piece from the inaugural celebration of the newborn prince. Every animal from all over the land journeys to witness the anointing of Simba to become the eventual successor. The next morning, after the ceremony's pomp and circumstance have passed, Simba awakens his sleeping father, eager to spend time alone with him and learn how to become a strong and wise king. After a little playtime, King Mufasa takes Simba to a high ridge and shows him the vastness of the land that will soon be his. He says

---

1   Henry Ward Beecher, *Life Thoughts: Gathered From the Extemporaneous Discourses of Henry Ward Beecher* (London, UK: Forgotten Books Classic Reprint, 2017).

to him, "Look, Simba, everything the light touches is our kingdom. A king's time as ruler rises and falls like the sun. One day, Simba, the sun will set on my time here, and will rise with you as the new king."[2]

Just from that scene alone, I could sense the majesty of the moment. I thought to myself, *What a noble and kind gesture for Mufasa to do that for his son, leaving him everything after he passes on.* It was a powerful scene that set the precedent for the rest of the movie, where we the audience get to have a front-row seat, witnessing the challenges Simba will face as he struggles in battle and ascends to the throne.

That scene with Simba and his father makes me think of myself. If you're a parent, perhaps you feel the same. What good parents wouldn't do that for their children? Of course, if you're the king and queen, it becomes your children's automatically as successors simply because of the royal bloodline. And everything that you are and everything that you own legally and legitimately becomes theirs as *rightful heirs to the throne and rulers of the kingdom.*

For context, I'm reminded of my travels as a business consultant. I've had the honor of traveling throughout this great and beautiful North American continent and have met a massive amount of wonderful people over the years. I am forever grateful for the generosity, kind words, and genuine love I've received from so many. As I've gotten to know a few of them better over time, true friendships formed, especially from those who have invited me into their homes. What stands out the most to me are the conversations we shared.

Most of these conversations were generally professional and usually related to business—that is, until the topic of their children came up. It's as if they had taken off a mask and revealed their true selves, or at least finally talked about a subject that engaged them. I've watched how smiles came across their faces when describing something their kid did, a class or club they joined, or some other worthy achievement. It didn't matter what it was. These were proud parents, to say the least. If you were to ask them what they wanted to see their kids do or become in the future—what their hopes and dreams were—not one time did I hear a parent say a negative or bad word about the aspirations they had for them. Of course, as parents, it's not uncommon to express dis-

---

2   *The Lion King*, dir. Roger Allers and Rob Minkoff, Walt Disney Pictures, 88 mins. (1994).

appointment from time to time when we think our children are not tapping into their full potential or offer a retort when we sense they're getting off track or hanging with the wrong crowd. But that doesn't mean we're ashamed or embarrassed to be their parents. In fact, in life all over the globe, regardless of economic status, I'll bet you can find parents who are enthusiastically invested in wanting their kids to aspire to be better than they were and even better than their grandparents.

Some see these aspirations as honoring and appreciating those who have sacrificed before them so that their children can have a better life than they did—a more productive, successful, happier, and fulfilled life. Nothing unusual about that at all. In the same way, I think it's rare you'll hear a child say that they want to be a deadbeat or a waste of time and energy or poor when they grow up.

Why do humans aspire? Why does it matter so much to parents to want their kids to do better in life and become all they were created to be? And why do kids want to fulfill their wishes by trying to become something great themselves? Where does all this zeal and aspiration for our offspring come from? Some would say it's natural, it's a paternal instinct, or, in the spirit of *The Lion King*, it's the circle of life!

Before becoming a parent of three amazing children, I'll never forget the morning my wife and I woke up at around the same time to talk about growing our family. It was a bright Saturday morning in Texas, and I rolled over to face her and asked, "What's on your mind?"

She said with a smile, "What's on *your* mind?" A little nervous, I said, "I was thinking about us, you and me, adding to our family. I think I'm ready to be a dad!"

Her response surprised me. She said with excitement, "Oh, my gosh! I was thinking the same thing!" Then I replied, "Oh, you want to be a dad, too?" Of course, I couldn't help but poke fun, because I didn't expect that response and I was still kind of nervous about the idea. But knowing we were in agreement and wanted the same thing at that moment calmed my nerves and boosted my excitement!

I'm recalling this part of our life because I won't ever forget the thought and effort we put into preparing for our first child's arrival. I remember feeling so proud and nervous at the thought of being a father, long before they were even born. Just knowing my beautiful wife was pregnant was so surreal. If you're a parent, you probably know exactly what I'm describing. Every thought and action was in anticipation of our new addition to the family. *What will we name them? What will they look like? Will it be a boy or girl? How much will they weigh? We'll need a car seat, baby carriage, diapers, college fund, and....* You get the idea. Although it was exciting and scary at the same time, we were certain of one thing and we knew it without question: We would love them! Even before they were born, regardless of anything, whether sick or healthy, boy or girl, we knew we would love them. It was just a natural thing.

Coincidentally, in the first book of the Bible, we see a happy parent, the Creator of all, also awaiting the arrival of His firstborn. Over the centuries, volumes of books and deep thinkers have asked and pondered the question, "Why were we created?" Yet, I find the answer to be naturally simple: God wanted a family. He desired to create something like Himself, by Himself, and for Himself. (If you were looking for a deeper answer, then you're welcome to explore.) For me, simply wanting a family is not beyond the unthinkable. All living things can procreate and most humans on the planet have a desire to, and this isn't too hard for me to accept as truth. The pattern for existence is all around us, but I can see why it's hard for some to believe—partially because, intellectually, it's a simple answer to a very complex hypothesis. I get it.

Human existence is such a complicated study that to explain it all by saying God created us because He wanted to co-exist with His very own creation can be too elementary for the advanced modern mind. Instead, there must be some deeper, more enigmatic explanation with a much larger truth. It's possible, but is there any proof? Let's look at nature.

Look around you and see how nature expresses itself through creation. Anything and everything that can produce life produces itself after its kind—molecules, microorganisms, plants, animals, and people. Simply put, we desire to have children for the same reasons that God wanted children. It's hardwired into our spiritual DNA to procreate and extend our existence. And like a good parent, God desires that those He calls His children also progress and succeed in every capacity, as they were designed and created to do.

WHY THIS MATTERS

This explanation from the Bible gives us a license to explore. When something is created, it is not the responsibility of the thing created to provide for itself; instead, the responsibility falls on the one who created it. Look in the book of Genesis and focus on what it says in Genesis 1:26–28 (Common English Bible, or CEB): "Then God said, 'Let us make humanity in our image to resemble us so that they may take charge of the fish of the sea, the birds in the sky, the livestock, all the earth, and all the crawling things on earth.' God created humanity in God's own image, in the divine image God created them, male and female, God created them. God blessed them and said to them, 'Be fertile and multiply; fill the earth and master it. Take charge of the fish of the sea, the birds in the sky, and everything crawling on the ground.'" Notice that God did not *speak us into existence* as He did with the rest of creation listed in Genesis 1:1–25. Instead, He created us out of Himself! Just as we create other humans out of ourselves from the seeds within us, God birthed us out of Himself from what He is made of, which is spirit, not flesh. Since we were created out of Him, we are then like Him. But the responsibility for provision falls on the shoulders of God the Creator, not the creation He made. This is why He created and supplied everything for man in the days before man existed.

Looking back to when my wife and I wanted to grow our family, not one time did we think that when the baby comes, they would have to provide for themselves. In fact, before their arrival, we'd already supplied everything they could ever need! Other loving and generous people overwhelmed us with more gifts and supplies, simply because they were as excited for us as we were for ourselves. This was a human example of the creators providing for the thing they created. Even if we were poor, there was nothing that we wouldn't have done to make certain that our children had whatever they needed to grow, develop, and mature into becoming functioning adults who eventually could provide for themselves. If we were wealthy, it would be no different. Our wealth would be their wealth simply because they were born out of us and carried our name. In the same way, because the Creator of all has created all things, including you and me, then what He has created is obliged to be abundantly supplied for, even after it can supply for itself. Likewise, if the creator is wealthy, the creation is automatically wealthy. If the parents are royal, then the children are automatically royal. Like Mufasa and Simba, the child is royal and wealthy simply because they were created by wealthy and royal parents.

Let's look at that passage again and focus on verse 26. It reads, "Let us make humanity in our image to resemble us." "Let us" means the Trinity of Himself: the Father, the Son, and the Holy Spirit—the Eternal Mind, the Spoken Word, and the Power of All Action. The word "image" means to picture or represent in the mind. The word "resemble" means to be a likeness, to appear or function in the same way. If you were made by the Creator of All in His likeness, then that means you are to think, speak, and function like the Creator Himself, which is your intended function based on His original design.

If we are made like the Creator of All and we're supposed to think, speak, and function like Him, then what is He and how does He think, speak, and function? The answers to these questions moving forward will serve as key foundational truths that will help you learn how to unlock an abundant supply that fulfills every need and want you can possibly imagine and manifest it into your life by divine design.

YOUR NATURE

As a person, you are created in three parts—body, soul, and spirit—yet you are called man and womb-man, or woman—that is, the man with the womb. The core of what you are, and this is the most powerful part of you, is the *invisible* part—your spirit man. This is your creation center or manufacturing headquarters. Everything that is created and manifested into this earth's three-dimensional realm comes from the spirit realm in thought, then travels through the soul. Desires, vision, thoughts, and concepts are all conceived spiritually and then manifested or brought to physical existence in the earth by being formed or made. Let's look at each.

YOUR BASE NATURE

Your body is your lower self. Your physical form is composed of living cells and extracellular materials, and organized into tissues, organs, and systems. It's the physical substance that makes up humans. Chemically, the human body consists mainly of water and organic compounds—i.e., lipids, proteins, carbohydrates, and nucleic acids. The human body is about 60% water by weight.[3]

We need this vessel, or earth suit, in order to function within earth's three-dimensional environment. Without it, we would not have physical form. Society places a lot of time, energy, and resources on the interworking and function of the body, using exercise, nutrition, and research to keep it healthy and operating smoothly. Unfortunately, one day this part of you will give out, decay, die, and return to the source from which it was formed—the dust of the ground.

YOUR CENTRAL NATURE

Your soul is your central self. It is the go-between for your body and your spirit. It houses the five senses—taste, touch, smell, sight, and hearing. It is how you form your voice and speech, and process your thoughts, emotions, will, and intellect. The soul is defined as a person or the essence of a person. It's the part of you that makes you who you are and will live on after your body expires within your spirit.

The soul is also where most people focus their lives by determining direction and making decisions according to knowledge, stimulated emotions, and logic. As with the body, tons of research and resources are dedicated to understanding more about this part of man. Libraries, universities, and science labs have all been created through research, understanding, and discovery. We know the soul exists because it gives the body life. When the body dies, the soul of you continues to live and moves on to another dimension.

YOUR SUPER NATURE

Your spirit is your higher self. This is what you are made of. It's the part of you that's connected to the soul and gives it life. While the two, soul and

---

3 "The Water in You: Water and the Human Body," United States Geological Survey (USGS), accessed August 9, 2021, https://www.usgs.gov/special-topic/water-science-school/science/water-you-water-and-human-body?qt-science_center_objects=0#qt-science_center_objects.

spirit, are often used interchangeably, the primary distinction between soul and spirit in man is that the soul is the animate life, or the seat of the senses, desires, affections, and appetites. The spirit is that part of you that connects, or refuses to connect, to God. It's the seat or core from where all thoughts, desires, and provisions flow in order to draw all things back to you. Your spirit is like a vortex that creates thoughts and ideas that attract and magnetize those concepts out in the atmosphere, or realms of reality, and draws them back to you, whether good or bad. It's the most powerful part of your entire being, yet the most neglected. You can't feel or taste from your spirit. However, that part of you that just seems to *know*—in your gut, your heart, or that innermost part of you—is your spirit. It is this part of you that we will explore and explain why wealth is already yours and why, by spiritual law, you have every right to possess whatever you need, when you need it, and as much as you are willing obtain.

It is when these three parts of you are working in harmony or synchronicity with one another that you are operating in your original design. However, if only two of the three are in operation, you'll experience hits and misses, trials and errors, wins and losses, and emotional ups and downs. That's not God's original intent for your life, yet He will use all of it to guide you to your destiny. It's built-in that you are designed to profit.

CHARACTERISTICS OF GOD

It's important that we understand the God part of who and what we are. Anything that does not know its reason for existence cannot function from its original design or intent, nor can it reach its highest potential. People are limited based on ignorance. They lack because they don't know or understand what they already have. Therefore, they look outward rather than inward for provision and wealth.

Ignorance of what you are will ultimately cause frustration, which leads to misuse and misunderstanding, which causes operational malfunctions and is then rendered useless. If I owned an Apple iPhone, for example, and thought it was designed for hammering nails into wood, not only would I have wasted a lot of money and missed out on all the wonderful modern conveniences that its cutting-edge technology could provide, but I would also appear insane to anyone who would see me using it as a hammer and wonder why I was doing this. Furthermore, through my own ignorance, I probably would blame the manufacturer for misrepresentation. In the same way, a great number of people who operate and live life by only two-thirds of their created selves are oblivious to their God-given supernatural highest selves.

For context of the power you possess, let's look at the original intent behind your created self by studying the characteristics of the original creator or manufacturer of you, God. To try and describe God in His entirety would be an impossible task and an exercise in confusion and futility. However, He's been called the Universe, the God of All, the Omnipotent One, the Omniscient or All-Knowing Consciousness, the Great I Am, and so on. Although we can try and describe what God is, words cannot describe Him. But we can look at what the Bible says are His characteristics and discover our higher selves in the process.

GOD IS SPIRIT

John 4:24 (New King James Version, or NKJV) says that God is a spirit, and those who worship Him must worship in spirit and in truth. So, as we identified earlier, we know that God is spirit. Therefore, if we have been created from Him, this means that you and I are spirit also. The scripture goes on to say that whoever worships Him must do it in spirit. What does that mean? To worship is to show love and adoration for something. In religion, people throughout time have worshiped gods, other people, and things. Worship is an extreme form of love—it's a type of unquestioning devotion. If you worship God, then you love God so much that you don't question Him at all. This adoration is how you connect with God or become as one with Him, spirit to spirit.

One form of this connection is the kind a newborn baby makes with their mother: a natural but spiritual connection that's embedded within to nurture and receive nurturing. Another form is when a man and a woman become sexually intimate with one another. This form is the only type of connection where two people's spirits, souls and bodies all join together as one. Romans 8:8 (Amplified Bible Classic Edition, or AMPC) puts it this way: "So then, those who are living the life of the flesh [catering to the appetites and impulses of their carnal nature] cannot please or satisfy God or be acceptable to Him." In other words, you can't use the soul or the body to truly connect with God. It is only by spirit, because He is spirit.

God Is Light

Light illuminates; it reveals. Darkness is simply the absence of light. Just as we see with our soul by using sight, we can reveal or see by our spirit when we have vision to perceive. Sight is from the eyes; vision is from the spirit. It's vision that shows us what can be, whereas sight shows what is. Both are realities but are of different realms. 1 John 1:5 (New International Version, or NIV) describes Him this way: "God is light; in Him there is no darkness at all." As God is light, your core and inner being is also light.

God Is a Creator

God creates by thoughts, words, and actions. It's His nature. You are a creator also. You create by thoughts, words, and actions. The difference is that God creates from nothing and makes nothing into something. We create by taking something and *recreating* it into something else. This is why science and new discovery are so important to our lives in the soul realm. It is by the rules and laws of nature we can develop extraordinary things for the betterment of humanity, our environment, and our societies. However, this creativity can also be extremely dangerous, destructive, and even deadly when operating from a mind of darkness rather than light. Look again at the book of Genesis to see the trinity of God, which is thought, word, and action in operation.

Genesis 1:1–3 (NIV): "In the beginning God created [thought] the heavens and the earth. Now the earth was formless and empty, darkness was over the surface of the deep, and the Spirit of God was hovering [ready to act or activated] over the waters. And God said [formed the words of thought], 'Let there be light,' and there was light [manifested creation]." Evidence of this created form throughout the universe and all around us is known as matter. At the most fundamental level, matter is composed of elementary particles, known as quarks and leptons (the class of elementary particles that includes electrons).[4] Quarks combine into protons and neutrons, and

---

4   "Particle Physics," Simple Science, accessed August 9, 2021, https://www.imperial.ac.uk/humanities/webdesign/2012/nickyguttridge/html/page4.html.

along with electrons, form atoms of the elements of the periodic table, such as hydrogen, oxygen, and iron.[5] Science suggests that these quarks, like everything else, are made up of what has been described as vibrations,[6] thus confirming that when God speaks, that is the vibration of sound to make words—His energy is in all things. Colossians 1:17 (AMPC) puts it this way: "And He Himself existed before all things, and in Him all things consist [cohere or are held together]." Along with matter, there's space and time. This is confirmed in Genesis that the universe is all space, all time, and all matter. In fact, many scientists speak of the entire universe as a space-time-matter continuum.

GOD IS GOOD

He cannot be evil. There is no evil in Him. It is vital to your understanding that you know, believe, and trust that God is only good! As darkness is the absence of light, evil is the absence of good. Often when tragedy strikes, some people believe it's God doing it, but it's not God.

GOD IS LOVE

God cannot hate. When connected to Him, you are love also. 1 John 4:7–8 (Amplified Bible, or AMP) says it like this: "Beloved, let us [unselfishly] love and seek the best for one another, for love is from God; and everyone who loves [others] is born of God and knows God [through personal experience]. The one who does not love has not become acquainted with God [does not and never did know Him], for God is love." To know God is to know love.

We've all probably had experiences where expressions of love were shown or demonstrated and have benefited from receiving generosity of what we call love. But to say that God *is* love means that love, in itself, is not an expression. When something is, it's then a noun, not a verb. Love is God. And to know Him, you must first experience Him.

---

5   Tim Sharp, "What is an atom? Nucleus, protons and electrons," Live Science, September 11, 2019, https://www.livescience.com/37206-atom-definition.html.

6   "Big Questions: Superstrings," NASA, accessed August 17, 2021, https://imagine.gsfc.nasa.gov/science/questions/superstring.html.

God Is a Giver

You can read passages of scripture throughout the Bible where the giving nature of God is expressed. Psalms 29:11 says He gives strength. Psalms 37:4 says He gives the desires of your heart. He gives grace and glory in Psalms 84:11. He gives what is good, according to Psalms 85:12. It says He gives perseverance and encouragement in Romans 15:5. He gives life to all things, according to 1 Timothy 6:13. He gives us the victory through our Lord Jesus Christ in 1 Corinthians 15:57.

Again, as a parent to a child, He gives. In Luke 12:32, Jesus says, "Do not be afraid, little flock, for your Father has been pleased to give you the kingdom." Verses 1 John 5:14–15 (NIV) go on to establish this point even further by saying, "This is the confidence we have in approaching God: that if we ask anything according to His will, He hears us. And if we know that He hears us—whatever we ask—we know that we have what we asked of Him." Notice it says, "whatever we ask" and then says "we know" we have it. Even a child could understand this simple premise. As long as a child has confidence in knowing that the parent loves them, they are not afraid to approach them and ask for stuff. Why? Because they are supposed to. Instinctively they know where all provisions come from, and they have no need to try and produce those provisions themselves. As the parent, if you love what you've created, you'll try and get stuff for them. As long as it is something that won't harm them, it doesn't even have to be a need.

There is a reason why children love toys. They don't need them; they simply want them. Toys allow children to be creative while they play with them. I've seen parents stand in long lines, sleep outside of department stores, empty their savings, and sometimes borrow to simply fill their child's request of something they wanted. They do this because they love them, they are givers, and it's their God-like nature to do so.

God Rules

The passage 2 Chronicles 20:6 (NIV) says, "Are you not the God who is in heaven? You rule over all the kingdoms of the nations. Power and might are in your hand, and no one can withstand you." God rules, and he's given man the same mantle of dominion. Genesis 1:26 (CEB) reads, "Let us make humanity in our image to resemble us so that they may take charge...."

Yes, the characteristics of God are in every person, including the desire to take charge or rule something. And it's by this understanding that everything you are created to be is to operate like God intended. The second letter of Peter, or 2 Peter 1:3–4 (NIV), says it this way: "His [God's] divine power has given us everything we need for a godly life through our knowledge of Him who called us by His own glory and goodness. Through these, He has given us His very great and precious promises, so that through them you may participate in the **divine nature**..."

This text says a lot. His divine power has been given to us for everything that we need to live a godly or God-like life through knowing His glory, which is light, and goodness. This is achieved through His promises and by using your divine or super nature in harmony with His, like parent and child.

I believe that, as children while we were in the presence of our parents, regardless of the views we've adopted over the years about them, not many of us wondered about the country's economy or if we would one day not have clothes to wear or food to eat. We knew they would somehow provide for us. So, why do so many question whether God will provide?

I've heard many ministers speak boldly proclaiming that God will meet your needs, even the Bible says so in Philippians 4:19 (NIV): "And my God will meet all your needs according to the riches of His glory in Christ Jesus." But does that mean God won't supply your wants also? If this is to be believed, then why do we have wants and desires in the first place? Are wants to be ignored or stuffed down deep within us because perhaps wanting is some form of lustful desire? Is it wrong to want anything above our needs? If so, why do so many aspire to achieve? Why do we praise and in some instances follow the wealthy or high achievers? In these next few chapters, I hope to shed some light on our divine nature and why, in my opinion, having wealth is a God-given right and not just a noble ambition. I also want to expand on what I believe is the root cause of poverty, why some are imprisoned with this mindset, and why breaking free from its stronghold is vital for building wealth and living a life of purpose and true fulfillment.

CHAPTER 2

LIKE KIND PRODUCES KIND

"A new type of thinking is essential if mankind is to survive and move toward higher levels."

—Albert Einstein

When living in California, we got to know a man who became a good family friend. (We'll call him Doug for purposes of anonymity.) Our friendship grew over a span of a few years. Doug was a jovial guy with a great sense of humor, but he was not someone who had a positive outlook on life. He thought of himself as someone who never seemed to catch a break. For example, if something positive was supposed to happen for him on Monday, by Tuesday it had fallen apart.

Most of our conversations were positive and uplifting, though, mostly because I was the one doing the encouraging. However, as my time away from him would separate us, he would eventually go right back to the doldrums. When this happened, he'd isolate himself and wouldn't take my calls. This went off and on for quite some time. He would always share with me what he wanted to do with his life, but he could never seem to get the right connections, save enough money, or make the right choices. He had embraced and accepted hopelessness as his lot in life. One day, my wife and I decided we were going to help him.

One of his desires was to have his own lawn service company. Upon hearing this, my wife and I came together and decided along with a few others that we would buy him all the equipment he would need for a lawn business and present it to him on his birthday. More than that, I put my selling and business development skills to work and even landed a couple of accounts in advance to help get him started. As planned, we presented everything to him on his birthday. As he looked at all the new equipment and the people who came together to make this all happen for him, he felt overwhelmed. He was filled with emotion and gratitude. He knew who had put this whole thing in motion, so he asked us what he could do to show his appreciation. We simply responded, "Just do well and be successful." He said that wasn't enough, so I asked him to service my yard at no charge. Had I not gotten the accounts for him before he got started, I would have gladly paid for his services.

It wasn't that long into his new business that he began to slack off—not showing up on the days he said he would, cutting back on some of his services, charging different prices to customers depending on how he felt about them, and getting a little contentious with them, too. I asked him what was going on, and he said it was because of his car. Carrying the equipment in his car was tough, and his car was old and needed a ton of repairs. To remedy that situation, when we were leaving California and moving back to Texas, my wife and I gave him our newer car as a departing gift. Again, he was emotionally overwhelmed and grateful.

Years later, Doug's business never grew and is today non-existent. The car got trashed, and he never fixed it. Though we heard from him a few times out of a year, including our visit to California to witness his marriage, circumstances got worse and no words of encouragement could pull him out. He was later divorced. He stopped reaching out to us and cut off all future communication. To this day, Doug doesn't talk to us anymore.

I don't tell you this story to air out differences. Rather, I tell it to show that life can be hard, things happen, and even with the greatest of intentions and ambitions, some things don't work out the way we had hoped. As you were reading this story about our relationship with him, you may have been thinking to yourself, *But it was his attitude. The guy clearly had an unhealthy outlook to life and didn't possess the character and savvy to make a better life for himself. It's his own fault.* Or maybe it was his education, or lack thereof. (He did attend college, by the way.) Or could it have been the people he associated himself with? (Well, he did associate with me.) Or maybe the guy just really couldn't catch a good break in life. While this is only one personal account of someone not seeming to get his life on track, there are so many more like Doug.

In 2017, I came across an interesting article, written by Joan Maya Mazelis, an assistant professor of sociology and an affiliated scholar at the Center for Urban Research and Education at Rutgers University-Camden. She had also written a book called, *Surviving Poverty: Creating Sustainable Ties among the Poor.*[7]

In her article, Mazelis points out that people who are labeled with a poverty mindset don't need to have a better attitude to escape poverty; instead, all of us should have a better attitude when it comes to poor people.[8] This was in response to a statement that Ben Carson, who was the secretary of Housing and Urban Development at the time, had made—that poverty is a state of mind and having the right mindset will let people escape poverty.[9] She argued that Carson's comments suggested a widespread misconception that poor people are poor because they aren't working hard enough and as a result of their own bad decisions.

Based on several interviews and her own research, she determined that even poor people agree with him. As an example, she interviewed a woman named Helen, a white woman in her 40s, who lived in a dilapidated house in Philadelphia with no running water. Although Helen and her husband both worked and were looking for better jobs with longer hours and higher pay,

---

7   Joan Maya Mazelis, *Surviving Poverty: Creating Sustainable Ties among the Poor* (New York, NY: NYU Press, 2017).

8   Joan Maya Mazelis, "Poverty really is a state of mind – among rich people," the *Washington Post,* June 20, 2017, https://www.washingtonpost.com/news/posteverything/wp/2017/06/20/poverty-really-is-the-result-of-a-state-of-mind-among-rich-people/.

9   Ibid.

she nonetheless agreed that poor people are lazy and don't want to work.[10] Mazelis said that she found in her research among Philadelphia's poorest residents that many believed that other poor people were lazy—but knew they themselves were not.

People working hard, yet they are still in poverty. How can this be? According to Statista.com, in 2019, 10.5% of the population were living below the poverty line in the United States,[11] which amounts to more than 34 million people according to population figures by the U.S. Census Bureau.[12] These numbers don't even include the damages a world pandemic may have caused. So, what's happening here in the United States and to people around the world? How is it possible for American citizens to live in such a rich and powerful country that is still recognized as one of the world's superpowers, yet they still struggle for survival and basic needs? In my opinion, regardless of whose side you choose—Mazelis's, Carson's, or Helen and her husband's—the answers are far deeper than simply a state of mind, economic policy, education, or lack of strong will to address the powers that hold so many in financial and economic bondage.

CORRUPTION BIRTHS CORRUPTION

I titled this chapter "Like Kind Produces Kind" because I believe it to be true. A corrupt and hopeless state of consciousness results in the birth of additional corruption. However, a good state of consciousness can birth goodness. You see, God created man in His image and likeness. Unfortunately, most of what we see today exists because created "gods" don't operate according to the Creator's specifications. Instead, they operate as mere humans and not from the place of their true, created spirit nature. And how can they when they've been born in corruption? Even though they are extremely powerful beings, they are still limited by a lack of connection to their source of life. No

---

10 Ibid.

11 "Poverty rate in the United States from 1990 to 2019," Statista, January 20, 2021, https://www.statista.com/statistics/200463/us-poverty-rate-since-1990/.

12 "QuickFacts: United States," United States Census Bureau, accessed August 9, 2021, https://www.census.gov/quickfacts/fact/table/US/PST045219.

matter the organism, when disconnected from its power or life source, it will malfunction and eventually die.

What we see today is not the Creator's original intent for man. People are confused about who, what, and why they were created, but are forever searching. It's a journey of finding meaning in life, purpose, and significance only few seem to find. Others come up empty—they are at a loss and have grown weary and given up the search altogether. They see themselves and life as a pointless and useless existence.

As of this writing, the suicide rate in the U.S. continues to rise.[13] Numbers from the Centers for Disease Control and Prevention show 47,511 people died by suicide in 2019, up from 47,173 two years prior.[14] While the increase was small, the rise in deaths over time has been steady. Since 1999, the suicide rate has climbed 35%.[15] Suicide is currently the nation's 10th leading cause of death, with 14.5 deaths per 100,000 people.[16] While thousands of people die by suicide each year, millions more think about it. In 2017, 10.6 million American adults seriously thought about suicide, 3.2 million planned it, and 1.4 million attempted it, according to the CDC.[17]

Additionally, ever notice the low regard some people have for life in general? How it seems they are just wasting it away with no direction, as if they're waiting for life's clock to expire? They abuse their bodies, poison their minds, and mangle and murder each other for small reasons or no reason at all. How stealing, rioting, lying, cheating, manipulating, fighting, and scheming are

---

13   Lea Winerman, "By the numbers: An alarming rise in suicide," *Monitor on Psychology* 50, no. 1 (January 2019), https://www.apa.org/monitor/2019/01/numbers.

14   "Suicide in Washington State," Forefront Suicide Prevention, accessed August 9, 2021, https://intheforefront.org/resources/suicide-data/.

15   Gaby Galvin, "The U.S. Suicide Rate Has Soared Since 1999," *U.S. News & World Report*, April 8, 2020, https://www.usnews.com/news/healthiest-communities/articles/2020-04-08/cdc-report-suicide-rate-up-35-since-1999.

16   "Underlying Cause of Death, 1999-2019 Results," Centers for Disease Control and Prevention (CDC), accessed August 9, 2021, https://wonder.cdc.gov/controller/datarequest/D76;jsessionid=FDF-D1A7293840A0C60484CFBF2EA.

17   "Suicide Prevention: Fast Facts," CDC, accessed August 9, 2021, https://www.cdc.gov/suicide/facts/index.html?CDC_AA_refVal=https%3A%2F%2Fwww.cdc.gov%2Fviolenceprevention%2Fsuicide%2Ffastfact.html.

the headlines we seem to read daily? We've gotten so used to hopelessness. Some of us try and escape reality by numbing the pain through some form of temporary pleasure. So much time, energy, and focus are placed on satisfying the body and the soul, but few give attention to their own spirit, the true power source of supply. How did the world become such a dark, scary, and seemingly undependable place? Perhaps it's been this way since the beginning.

THE ROOT OF EVIL

In the book of Genesis, chapter 3, we see the story of how man and woman were deceived by an evil serpent that caused them to rebel against what God had instructed them not to do. Once the plan was carried out successfully, the state of man and all mankind became infected with darkness, or the removal of God's presence. The light that once shined bright within them was unplugged from its main power source and eventually faded into darkness. Life was gone, and death entered in. Genesis 3:6–7 (NIV) says, "When the woman saw that the fruit of the tree was good for food and pleasing to the eye, and also desirable for gaining wisdom, she took some and ate it. She also gave some to her husband, who was with her, and he ate it. Then the eyes of both of them were opened, and they realized they were naked; so they sewed fig leaves together and made coverings for themselves." The part where it says, "…the eyes of both were opened…" means that their spiritual eyes dimmed and became dark while their soul eyes, the five senses, were opened. No longer did they navigate through life by wisdom, confidence, and vision, but instead by trial and error. For the first time, man fears God rather than reveres him, and the light and translucent appearance he once shared with God became fleshy. Mankind's light went out, and darkness reigned.

Where man was once completely and abundantly supplied for, he has now deemed himself as "god" and must provide for himself. Genesis 3:17–19 (NIV) says, "To Adam He said, 'Because you listened to your wife and ate fruit from the tree about which I commanded you, 'You must not eat from it,' cursed is the ground because of you; **through painful toil you will eat food** from it all the days of your life. It will produce **thorns and thistles** for you, and you will eat the plants of the field. **By the sweat of your brow you will**

eat your food until you return to the ground, since from it you were taken; for dust you are and to dust you will return.'" In other words, work, work, work, **sweat, and toil** for your own provision until you die. Since the beginning, man's primary motivation for doing most things in life is fear based: fear of not having enough, fear of being alone, fear of dying, fear, fear, fear and work, work, work.

Because of this disobedience to God, sin entered the heart of man and the earth became cursed. Plants and soil became cursed. Man feared animals when instead he was supposed to rule over them; he lost his position, his good standing with God, *and* his provision. Man began to believe he must now provide for himself. All of creation became cursed because of man. But what God spoke in Genesis 1:26, He never took away; man willingly gave away his position to the serpent. Now he and everything he produces will expire physically and eternally, known as death.

You see, you and I are free moral agents. We make choices and decisions for our own existence. Had God not given us free will, then we would not be made in His image and likeness. If you're wondering why the world is so dark and corrupt, it is simply the free will of every man making decisions without God's intervention. Up is now down, wrong is now right, and man now guides his life through knowledge and not wisdom—his base nature and not his given super nature.

The Hebrew word for knowledge is *daath*, which means to find out through experience, or a kind of conscious knowledge related to the soul.[18] Apart from God, we operate using trial and error, past experiences, logic, and intelligence. We feel our way through life as someone walking in darkness, yet we have no knowledge or indications of what the immediate future or next day will bring. We are led by our minds and not our spirit; we are not blessed but cursed. We only know the past and the present and have no inkling of the future; we can only guess. Possessing this state of blindness is the only way that we will ever look within ourselves to recognize that something is not right and that there must be more to life than this. We can sense a yearning that knocks on our hearts; we know that we are more and there is more. This

18   "Daath, the Door to Knowledge (1)," Glorian, accessed August 17, 2021, https://glorian.org/learn/courses-and-lectures/daath-the-tree-of-knowledge/daath-the-doorway-to-knowledge-1.

is how the search for meaning begins: an emptiness within us desiring to be filled.

Not knowing who or what you are can be dangerous, just like not knowing that electricity and water do not mix. Or not respecting the laws of physics such as gravity. Or simply not heeding the instructions from those in authority. Yes, what you don't know can hurt you and, in some cases, kill you. Man was doomed for eternal separation from God because of willfully siding with evil and darkness.

Whether you believe there is an inherent evil in existence or not is inconsequential. Fact is, no one can deny that life for most people can be a massive struggle, and many don't appear to come out on top. Altogether dismissing or ignoring the forces that work against us is the very reason why so many on the planet are not experiencing life the way it was meant to be lived. In the context of economics, living in poverty is not ideal, as is also true when living life with inherent evil.

Most Americans have likely not seen extreme poverty to the levels that are common in some areas of developing nations where basic human necessities like clean water and food are not always readily available. Starvation, disease, and death can be seen openly on the side of dirt roads and in the makeshift shelters they call home, for both children and adults. Many people I know who have traveled to such places and have witnessed these unimaginable sights up close have returned to this country with a completely different mindset for what hunger, insufficient healthcare, and lack of basic needs really are. They tell me the sights, sounds, and smells of such an existence are horrifying, heartbreaking, and hard to erase from their minds.

Many people wonder aloud, "How can a loving God allow such destruction and decay to exist, yet continue what He created and not address it?" Did God do this? Many believe so. But if you understand the nature and characteristics of what God is, you'll find the blame falls squarely on man and his choosing of free will and living life apart and in separation from Him—living by way of the senses and guided by a dark and confused mind, rather than by the light of the spirit within him. Then why won't God step in for the greater good and overrule man's will? If God were to impede your free will, then he would violate His own order, which would cancel out the image and likeness of Himself by which you were made and cause an eternal contradiction, thereby canceling everything created. Simply put, He cannot and will not violate His own laws.

The stars and galaxies exist and do what they have been created to do. Plant and animal species exist, grow, and re-create without man's influence or interruption. Why is it that we humans seem to be the only creation on earth that can't seem to connect the dots or function the way we were intended? We can't because man turned away from light and embraced the darkness as a way for life, and he had the free will to choose it. Therefore, it is this attachment and influence of evil that is allowed to reign and control the things in our lives, because we willingly partner with forces and principles that are in direct contrast to what God has ordained and ordered.

Consequently, no matter how hard you try and no matter how hard you work, even with the best intentions, you are no match against the evil spiritual forces that rule the world while battling in this base natural state of consciousness. It's the legal transference of power and rule from man to darkness and principles of the curse operating on this earth that began from the fall of man. To see an example of it in today's world, look to Helen and her husband, who work extremely hard every day yet still live in poverty. Consider my friend Doug, who couldn't seem to get a break when I knew him. It's likely that his life today is no different. Perhaps you or people you know just can't seem to pull it together no matter how hard you or they are trying. Perhaps you get some small victories every now and then, but nothing life changing. I've been there and have seen all sides of not having enough.

I had a normal childhood growing up. I was raised in a modest family with a mom and a dad, and I'm the middle child of five. If you're a middle child, you know what that's like. You're too old for what the younger siblings get to enjoy, or you're too young for what the older siblings get to do. My brother was the eldest child, so usually clothes were handed down to me when he grew out of them. Sure, I had my share of nice things, but for the most part I had to share them or wait for something to be shared. The neighbors' kids were my friends, and we all grew up together while attending public school.

As a kid, I don't remember too many tough times, because it never seemed that way. It was just our way of life. When we wanted something, we asked for it. If we were told no, we became resourceful and looked for ways to get it on our own by mowing lawns, bagging groceries, or whatever it took if it was desired enough. We knew everything had its limits, so that was normal. My dad worked as a diesel mechanic, and in the 1960s and 1970s he did pretty well for himself. He was a Vietnam veteran who didn't get the hero's welcome when returning home, but that never deterred him from wanting to make his dream of one day owning his own business come true. My mom, on the other hand, was mostly home with us, but also did odd jobs to help out. She married young, at 17.

She kept an exceptionally clean home and was a proud wife and mother, but that didn't last. My parents divorced when I was 12, and all five of us kids lived with our mother. Things really changed. We didn't get new cars every five or six years like before. When things around the house broke, like air-conditioning units or washers and dryers, it wasn't easy to replace them. In most cases, we just did without. Somehow, we didn't miss many meals, although some items on the menu changed.

We all had to pitch in when we could, so I learned a lot about labor and paying bills at an incredibly young age. When my mother was growing up, she was pulled in and out of school to help her parents in the fields, which stunted her education. She only completed her schooling up to the sixth-grade level. But what she lacked in education, she certainly made up in wisdom and tenacity. She was a survivor. And she knew she had to pull together her best resources—her children—in order to make it.

Because of a lack of education, she couldn't read that well, so at a young age, I had to learn quite a bit about mortgages and amortization schedules, utility bills and insurances, and past-due notices and welfare applications—all while going to middle school and high school. It was in high school during an economics class that I learned we were poor. Since I helped manage the bills, I knew what we had coming in and going out. According to results of the March 1981 Current Population Survey (CPS) conducted by the Bureau of the Census, the American median family income was $21,020. The poverty income guideline for that month in 1981 was $7,480.[19] We were right at the poverty line.

QUEST FOR SOMETHING GREATER

Although this was a revelation to me, I never felt poor. As a family, we had a lot of laughter and love in our home. We lived in a decent neighborhood. We had our fights, too, but we always knew it would blow over and things would go back to normal. Both my mom and dad had a wonderful sense of humor. Perhaps this is how they coped. Regardless, their lightheartedness was certainly passed down to their children. We just never looked at any situation as complete doom and gloom, and that was the end. We knew we would overcome somehow if we just persevered.

Furthermore, they taught us faith. There was always a sense of knowing that no matter how bad things seemed, somehow it would work itself out—perhaps not when we wanted it to, but nevertheless it did. My dad instilled in me an understanding and awareness that we are not alone in this world and that we always have help in times of trouble if we call out to God. Well, these were certainly troubled times, so where was He? Why did my parents fight so much? What caused their divorce? Why were we in such bad economic shape with barely enough to get by? These questions fueled my quest to find God.

While my friends in high school enjoyed life as teenagers through sports, music, dating, and so on, my time and thoughts were occupied with survival for my sisters, my mom, and me. I went to school during the day and work during nights and weekends. Even though I was doing what I could, my mom was not always appreciative of it. She was clearly a hurt and bitter person after the divorce. How could she not be? She had placed her future and hopes in a person she trusted to love, honor, and support her, but it hadn't worked out as planned. Sometimes her anger and pain spilled out on us.

Of course, I didn't understand it at that age, so, yes, there was tension. Although I wanted to leave, I couldn't see myself abandoning the mess my dad had left us in. It made me feel as if I would have been no different than he

---

19   "Characteristics of the Population Below the Poverty Level: 1980," U.S. Department of Commerce, July 1982, https://www2.census.gov/library/publications/1982/demographics/p60-133.pdf.

was. And I refused to be like he was because of it. I took the good things about him with me mentally and shunned the bad. I figured I would forge my own path my own way and would far exceed anything he'd ever done. So, I went on a quest through religion to find answers.

I started with Buddhism, because it is also a major global religion. During my search, I learned that Four Noble Truths comprise the essence of Buddha's teachings, though I felt that there is quite a bit that is very confusing, contradictory, and left unexplained. The four truths include the truth of suffering, the truth of the cause of suffering, the truth of the end of suffering, and the truth of the path that leads to the end of suffering.[20] I also learned that Karma is not like it's commonly explained today. In Buddhist interpretation, Karma does not refer to some preordained payback or fate. Instead, it refers to good or bad actions a person makes during their lifetime.[21] Furthermore, there are different realms of rebirth a person can be born into. But I didn't learn exactly how this worked, only that we had to reach Nirvana, or spiritual bliss.[22] Since I was already suffering, I wasn't looking for more of it. So, I left the practice.

Next, I researched Judaism. I found Judaism to be closely related to much of what I read in the Old Testament of the Christian Bible, but I found the practice to be systematic. A lot of emphasis is placed on community and its members. However, there were many levels to becoming accepted or affirmed as one of their own in the faith.[23] I thought to myself, *Why does a person have to qualify through rituals and ordinances to be accepted by God?* This was something I was willing to commit to, but it was also confusing to me. Perhaps there was a deeper answer to these questions, but I didn't stick around to ask.

I then investigated Catholicism. This too was short-lived. After some discourse with a priest, who insisted I acknowledge him as Father, he got angry

---

20   "The Four Noble Truths," BBC Religions, updated November 17, 2009, https://www.bbc.co.uk/religion/religions/buddhism/beliefs/fournobletruths_1.shtml.

21   Joseph Goldstein, "Cause and Effect: Reflecting on the law of karma," *Tricycle* (2008), https://tricycle.org/magazine/cause-and-effect/.

22   "What does Buddhism teach about life after death?" BBC Bitesize, accessed August 9, 2021, https://www.bbc.co.uk/bitesize/guides/zfts4wx/revision/3.

23   Tzvi Freeman, "Why Is Conversion to Judaism so Hard?" Chabad, accessed August 9, 2021, https://www.chabad.org/library/article_cdo/aid/3002/jewish/Why-Is-Conversion-to-Judaism-So-Hard.htm.

with me because I asked him why the Vatican seems to change the rules periodically depending on issues. I wasn't out of line in my questioning. Catholics generally recognize that many (if not all) Catholic moral teachings on specific issues belong to the category of non-infallible teachings. In other words, many moral issues are open for reinterpretation and rethinking. In fact, John L. Allen Jr. wrote in his piece "Think Again: Catholic Church" that Catholics who have been around the block know that whenever someone in authority begins a sentence with, "'As the church has always taught …,' some long-standing idea or practice is about to be turned on its head."[24] To me, truth is truth and should therefore stand the test of time. Does God change His mind? If so, does He give us a warning or a heads-up? Who could follow this? I knew I couldn't. My search for meaning and purpose was frustrating and seemed hopeless, but I wasn't up to the challenge of trying to fight this battle called life on my own. I'd seen too many lose it.

---

24   John L. Allen Jr., "Think Again: The Catholic Church," *Foreign Policy*, October 1, 2009, https://foreignpolicy.com/2009/10/01/think-again-the-catholic-church/.

CHAPTER 3

THE WAY OF TRUE WEALTH

"Submit to God and be at peace with him, in this way
prosperity will come to you."
—*Job 22:21 (NIV)*

High school was a conundrum for me. I excelled in my studies when I wanted to, but I had trouble connecting the dots of what I was learning and how it applied to the reality of my life. And if I couldn't figure it out, how was that going to change anything in my future?

I didn't hang out with the wrong crowd. I didn't experiment with drugs or drinking. But I did have a sense of humor that got me into trouble at times. I found humor in some of the darkest situations. I cracked jokes, acted silly, and got in trouble. It did get me attention, though, especially from the ladies.

My first girlfriend and I talked a lot on the phone after school. In fact, that's all we could do. I was bused from across town, from the lower- to middle-income parts of Houston down South. She lived West, in the slightly higher-income parts of Houston. I didn't have a car, so we could only see each other at school. During the summer, we broke up. I felt relieved, because the pressure of trying to be a boyfriend with no car was tough. Sure, girls had cars, too, but the last thing I needed was to be revealed as the fun guy who was poor. I worked and bought my own clothes for my younger sisters and me, but the house was something I couldn't hide. So, we met at different places. After a few girlfriends here and there, I no longer wanted to date anymore. Besides, it all seemed pointless to me if it wasn't going anywhere.

At this point in my life, I was seeking. I looked at others and wondered if they were experiencing the same void I was and what they were doing to fill it since I couldn't seem to find an escape. Eventually, I turned back to the faith my dad taught me, remembering how he had told me that God was always there in times of trouble. I certainly felt troubled, but where was He? The people in my life who claimed to know God were people who drank, smoked, partied, cursed, cheated on their spouses, neglected their children, and worked hard while hating their jobs and barely getting by. Sure, they had modest homes and American-made cars. But I just couldn't see where God made this big difference in their lives compared to those who had never claimed to know God, except when they said they knew they were going to Heaven when they die. *When they die? What about living here on earth?* I thought.

THE CASE FOR JESUS

Death is inevitable. It's the only guarantee we have. Even as a young man, I knew this to be true. And it scared me. I didn't like the thought of dying because it seemed so final, and no one seemed to know exactly what would happen afterwards. I thought life was already hard enough on earth. *You mean to tell me there's more pain coming?* With that in mind, I remembered how my dad always assured me that if I was saved, that is, if I accepted Jesus, death would no longer be something to fear. In fact, it would be something to embrace. He was confident in this.

As I got closer to graduating high school, I tried to figure out what I was going to do with my life. Everyone else seemed to have it all mapped out. They were going off to college to get their degrees and join the workforce at some major corporation. A part of me was envious. They seemed to have some direction for their lives, and they knew what they wanted to do. Quite frankly, I didn't.

High school was somewhat of a safe haven for me. It gave me structure for my days. I knew where I was supposed to be, what I was supposed to do, and who my friends were. I had a part-time job at a grocery store after school that helped me pay for a few things I wanted while helping my mom. If nothing else, I thought, I'd make it a career if I had to. After all, grocery managers, general managers, and store directors seemed to do pretty well for themselves. But that's not exactly what I wanted to do. I didn't know what I wanted to do, but I sure knew what I didn't want to do. College didn't seem plausible because tuition was so expensive. I certainly couldn't afford it with my part-time pay, and the thought of wasting that kind of money while trying to figure it out seemed absurd. Life seemed bleak.

So, I figured, I'd better get this salvation thing out of the way, but I wasn't exactly sure how to do that either. All I knew was that I needed to accept Jesus into my life and get baptized. So, I did that, but nothing really changed from what I could tell. I wanted to go to church more often, but that was mostly because I thought Jesus wouldn't like it if I didn't. My mom had the only car in our home, and she would only let me use it for work. She had no interest in church during those times and wanted nothing to do with it, so asking to borrow her car for church was out of the question. I went on my own using public transportation.

After graduating high school, I held on to my grocery job. I figured I would work to move up, but it seemed the harder I tried, the more elusive it became. All I wanted to do was save enough money to get my own car, which seemed impossible between the low wages and paying rent to stay with my mom. I was angry at my mom. If I had to use the small amount I brought in to pay her rent, how on earth would I ever be able to save up for a car? Then my anger was redirected at my dad. Had he not divorced my mom, we wouldn't be in this predicament. More accurately, *I* wouldn't be in this predicament.

But I was a churchgoer now, and that wasn't the right attitude I was supposed to have. One of the Ten Commandments says to honor your father and your mother, for this is right in the sight of God. I reasoned that leaving my mom's place and finding my own probably wouldn't be the best thing financially. The amount of money I would need to rent an apartment would certainly be higher than what she was asking for every month. So, I figured this was better economically, and I continued to catch public transportation to church.

After high school, there were only a couple of people I stayed in contact with. One was a close friend I secretly wanted to date. I'll call her Grace. When I finally got the nerve to let her know how I felt, I learned she didn't like me that way. But soon she tried to set me up with someone else. This young lady was her best friend, she told me. She was convinced we would be perfect together. But after Grace had rejected me, I figured I had bigger issues in my life to work out. Death was covered, but this living economically at the poverty line thing wasn't. But Grace persisted, even when her friend told her she was interested in a guy she'd seen at her local grocery store. I thought it was all set to go away until I realized the guy at the grocery store was *me*.

Grace told me her friend worked at the Sears, Roebuck and Company department store in downtown Houston, a place I rarely went. But one day my mom had to go there, so I tagged along. As soon as we got to the store, I separated from my family to see if I could catch a sneak peek from a distance. Grace had described what her friend looked like. After asking around, I learned she was on her lunch break.

When I finally saw her, she literally took my breath away. She was gorgeous. She had the most beautiful pair of eyes I'd ever seen and with a glowing smile to match. I was floored. We met, became friends, dated, and got married a year later. As of the writing of this book, we are still married. And she's even more beautiful now than she was then.

THE CURSE REVERSED

Everything was about to change for me, and the meeting of my future wife was pivotal. Yes, I was motivated to get a car before, but now I was *really* motivated. However, my financial status hadn't changed. Mom was still Mom, and the job still had not promoted me. A co-worker friend had often talked to me about joining the company's credit union as a member. She said if I signed up for their membership, they may help me get a vehicle.

Considering how little I was able to save from each paycheck, the numbers didn't seem to add up. She went on to tell me, "You don't need that much because you've been working here for a while. You know you need a vehicle," and on and on. I would just blow her off and say I'll get to it. This went on for weeks.

One day, she pretended she needed to borrow a few dollars because she didn't bring her wallet with her, so she asked me if I had $50 to lend her and she'd give it back to me the following day. I agreed because I knew she was an upstanding person, and besides that, she would have done it for me. We saw each other the next day, and instead of handing me the money I loaned her, she gave me a signature card with my name on it, showing I had opened an account from the credit union she kept lecturing me about. I looked at her perplexed and she said, "I'm doing you a favor because I know you won't do it for yourself. Give me a copy of your license, sign the card, have your checks direct deposited into the account, and keep it open for at least two weeks." She had this commanding way about her where you just did what she said. But she also had a good heart and knew in detail the struggles I was living with at home with my mom and in helping financially to keep us afloat. (In fact, most of my co-workers knew about my home life, as it was a running joke sometimes.) I knew she had my best interest in mind, so I went along with it and gave her everything she needed for my paychecks to be direct deposited into this new account.

As the weeks went by, I was still thinking about that credit union account I had opened. It gave me a little hope, even though I was still catching rides when I could and battling my mom to use her vehicle when I needed it. During that same time period, my dad called me. He asked if I wanted to grab lunch soon and go look at some vehicles. I hadn't told him anything about my wanting a car, so I thought it was odd he mentioned it.

Because of the divorce and an injury on his job that had left him somewhat disabled, I knew he was not able to buy a vehicle for me, let alone help me buy one, so I never thought for a second that was his reasoning for the visit. But he told me all about what kind of cars he thought were best to buy if I ever wanted to buy one. Remember, he was a diesel mechanic, so of course he had a few opinions about cars. I felt as if I heard something within me say, *Remember to always honor your father and your mother.* Later that day when I got home, I felt compelled to tell my mom I was sorry for being so angry about paying rent to live there. I went on to tell her that she wouldn't have to ask me for the money anymore, that I'd give it to her before she asked and without hesitation.

Fast-forward a couple of weeks later, *my friend from work* called me over. (By the way, I'm a big Marvel Cinematic Universe fan. Only you MCU nerds probably get that reference.) She reminded me that it had been a couple of weeks now, and I should make an appointment to go and talk with the credit union about purchasing a vehicle. Not believing any of it would happen, I did it anyway. At the credit union, they interviewed me, checked my records, told me to go out and find a vehicle, and handed me a form. That same day, I went to the place my dad and I had visited a few weeks before and asked the salesperson if the vehicle we had looked at then was still there. It was! That day, I bought my first car!

I couldn't believe it—no cosigners or a long-term loan, just a two-year loan with payments that were automatically deducted by the credit union. Based on the amount, it wasn't a stretch at all. After showing my girlfriend (my wife now), she was genuinely happy for me, because she knew how many times I either walked or caught public transportation.

How did this happen? I thought. Based on my calculations, it seemed there was no way I would have been able to accomplish this until years down the line. Despite my own doubts and logic, not getting a promotion, and paying rent, things just seemed to have worked out in a way that I could not have formulated on my own, considering the circumstances. A co-worker had opened an account for me, my dad had wanted to hang out and look at vehicles, which was strange, and I had heard that voice about honoring my parents. It all seemed connected somehow, and it came together in my favor.

Then it dawned on me. I remembered that in a moment of frustration and desperation one night, I had asked God that if he could somehow allow me to get a vehicle of my own, I would honor him and be in church every weekend. Could that have been what set this whole thing in motion? I wasn't sure, but I had my vehicle, I could see the woman I loved more often, and we both were in church every weekend.

You may be thinking, *People buy cars all the time, so what's the big deal?* For me, getting a car put in motion a deeper search for what God had to say about the things I needed in my life. I had never heard anyone say that God had made a way for them to get something like a car. I knew people who prayed and talked about what God did for them, but it always pertained to things like helping them cope with something emotionally, getting a loved one saved, or even asking for an attitude adjustment. Never for material things. According to the Christians I knew back in the day, you were supposed to abandon the desire for things in this world and only desire the things of God. Well, as far as I was concerned, I had "abandon things" covered by default because we were already lacking the worldly things. We were poor. And quite frankly, I didn't like it. There was nothing noble or honorable about it. It was a horrible way of life. So, I didn't think God was interested in providing stuff we needed or desired. But I asked for it anyway, and I got it.

The Bible says that Jesus came to save us and demonstrate God's great love for us. He came to show us who we are and the mess we have found ourselves in as His creation. Romans 5:19 (NIV) says, "For just as through the disobedience of the one man (Adam) the many were made sinners, so also through the obedience of the one man (Jesus) the many will be made righteous."

The entire Old Testament is really a chronicle of God looking for a man He could express himself through to ultimately redeem us from the curse that was brought in since the beginning. But he could not find one worthy, so He decided to do it Himself and come to us in the form of a man.

John 1:1–4 (NIV) says, "In the beginning was the Word, and the Word was with God, and the Word was God. He was with God in the beginning. Through Him all things were made; without Him nothing was made that has been made. In Him was life, and that life was the light of all mankind."

Then it continues in verses 11–14: "He came to that which was His own, but His own did not receive Him. Yet to all who did receive Him, to those who believed in His name, He gave the right to become children of God— children born not of natural descent, nor of human decision or a husband's will, but born of God. The Word became flesh and made His dwelling among us.

We have seen His glory, the glory of the one and only Son, who came from the Father, full of grace and truth."

During my research of different religions, none of them, except the Catholics, had the audacity to claim that God had sacrificed Himself to put us back in place with Him, for Him, and in our rightful standing. It was through His crucifixion, the pure and ultimate sacrifice of God himself, that you and I are now free—not just free to go to Heaven, but free from this earth's curse!

But let's look again at the story of His crucifixion and see what else Jesus did at the cross. We see movies about the depiction of His great sacrifice for the world, but they don't truly show the real work that was done for us.

During the events of the crucifixion, the Bible says in Matthew 27:28 (Contemporary English Version, or CEV): "They stripped off Jesus's clothes and put a scarlet robe on Him." This event was in direct relation to the depiction of when man gave his position away to the serpent in the garden in the beginning. Genesis 3:21 (CEV) says, "Then the Lord God made clothes out of animal skins for the man and his wife," because they were naked, afraid, and full of shame once their natural eyes were opened. This was never meant to be. The plan that the serpent convinced them of was reversed by Jesus when he replaced man's nakedness and shame with his own while suffering on the cross. Verse 29 says they then "twisted together a crown of thorns and set it on His head. They put a staff in His right hand. Then they knelt in front of Him and mocked Him. 'Hail, king of the Jews!' they said. They spit on Him and took the staff and struck Him on the head again and again." This was also an event that was necessary for removing the curse from the beginning for our own lack of provision that was caused by man when God said in Genesis 3:17–19 (Amplified Bible, or MP), "The ground is [now] under a curse because of you. In sorrow and toil you shall eat [the fruit] of it all the days of your life. Both thorns and thistles it shall grow for you; and you shall eat the plants of the field. By the sweat of your face you will eat bread until you return to the ground."

I believe the crown of thorns on his head is symbolic of Jesus taking that curse of lack and poverty to the grave with him also. The beating and mocking represent evil and darkness mocking us as we work day after day for food and things, knowing we will never make enough to relax because the ground is cursed. It will never produce enough for us and our families to stop working. I know what that feels like.

God did not wait until we got ourselves together, cleaned up and ready to present ourselves to Him, as if we could ever be good or clean enough to be accepted. God is perfect and pure. We are not. We are all under the same curse since the beginning. No good deeds done can ever remove it, just like no bad deeds we've done brings it on us. Unfortunately, we were all born this way, in rebellion and separated from God because we all came from the first man and woman after the curse had taken place.

But God has accepted us anyway because Jesus paid the penalty of judgment for us, opened the door, and paved the way back to God. The penalty of man's rebellion has been paid in full and is now canceled, no matter what you and I have done. God demonstrated His own love for us in this: While we were still sinners, Christ died for us and took the curse with Him. He spiritually placed us back in the garden, with full authority and all the benefits we had before the curse ever entered into our hearts and the earth, that is, if you have accepted His finished work as redemption for yourself.

CHAPTER 4

THE POWER OF TRUE WEALTH

*"I am the Lord your God, who teaches you to profit, who leads you
in the way that you should go."*

—*Isaiah 48:17 (AMP)*

My wife and I wed in our early 20s. Many people thought it was a bad idea, thinking we were too young. According to them, we had our whole life ahead of us. Marriage could wait. My reasoning to those sentiments was simply, *Exactly what life ahead of us were they speaking of?*

I knew in my heart this was the right thing to do, and she was the right one to do it with. She felt the same. I reasoned within myself that I had no ill intentions or surface motivations outside of enjoying her company and just wanting to be around her all the time. That was new and different. I had never felt that way about anyone. She was always encouraging and a wonderful listener. She would tell me about the gifts and talent that she saw within me, which were, quite frankly, things I couldn't see in myself. Over 35 years later, nothing has changed. We enjoy each other's company and are still each other's best friend. So much for the naysayers. But marriage in and of itself did not give me the inner peace I was still longing for, nor was it supposed to. The questions I had that still remained were, *What's my purpose in life, and will we always live a modest, substandard way of life?*

In my heart, I was determined to live a different life than the one I had growing up. Remember, a certain standard of living mattered to me because I knew what it felt like to live a life of minimal means. I did not want to raise a family in those same conditions, and I wanted to assure my new wife she married the right guy.

We leased our first apartment, and we both had cars. Our weekends were fun but were sometimes limited by our finances. During those early years, I worked for a bank, and my wife worked for an insurance firm. Our combined income afforded us to meet our needs and every now and then buy or do some things we wanted. Times were tough for many people. This was in the mid '80s, immediately after the recession era of 1981 to 1982.[25] Unemployment was a factor as some corporate layoffs were still happening.[26] So, we were grateful to have what we had.

We regularly went to church and genuinely cared about people. Interestingly, we met other young couples who were like us—newly married and involved in things of God. When I was growing up, it had been the older generation who were committed churchgoers. As for the younger people I knew then, church was never a topic of conversation or something of interest, unless it was brought up as some sort of punishment and that their parents made them attend. For me, going to church was okay, but it wasn't enough.

I was happy, but not content. Even though I had been baptized in high school, I was still not sure of where I'd go if I died, because salvation assurance was never taught or explained to me in detail. I just wasn't as terrified about it as I used to be, but I wouldn't reveal that openly. The only person I would express those thoughts to was my wife. Then things began to gradually

---

25   Tim Sablik, "Recession of 1981–82," Federal Reserve History, November 22, 2013, https://www. federalreservehistory.org/essays/recession-of-1981-82.

26   "As Economy Grew Since '83, Closings and Layoffs Took 9.7 Million Jobs," the *New York Times*, December 13, 1988, https://www.nytimes.com/1988/12/13/us/as-economy-grew-since-83-closings-and-layoffs-took-9.7-million-jobs.html.

shift around me, and from my perspective, it didn't appear as if circumstances were going to get better.

My wife, who at this point was not fully aware of whether she had accepted Jesus or not, would ask me questions about the Bible and ask for advice on what to tell her co-worker, who seemed to have had financial and relationship trouble. From what I understood at the time, her co-worker was a Christian.

My wife connected with her. After working hours, they talked quite a bit about the Bible. My wife would then come home with questions and ask about my thoughts on her perspective. Though my dad had taught me quite a bit about what he knew, I had never actually studied the Bible myself. Even though we were churchgoers, I wasn't always sure what the preacher was referring to. I just saw that people liked it and got quite excited about what was said, so I felt we were in a positive environment. I encouraged my wife to continue talking to her co-worker more, since she could explain some things and reference them directly from the Bible when I could not.

One night after I came home a little late from my bank job, my wife ran up to me and hugged me very tight as if she was relieved to finally see me. That was strange.

"What's wrong? Are you OK?" I asked.

She went on to explain that she had accepted what Jesus offered and felt different inside. So much so that when she looked in the mirror, it was as if she was seeing a completely different person and a glowing around her that kind of scared her.

I wasn't exactly sure what she was talking about, but deep down inside I knew my wife had changed. As best as I could explain it at the time, she had experienced something that I had not when I had accepted Jesus back in high school. I was happy for her, but I couldn't help but wonder what went wrong with me. *What happened to her that didn't happen for me? Was I rejected? Did I do something that God didn't like, so my request was denied? What happened?* It was weird, but I knew we were different as a couple. I was convinced that she had been accepted, and I had been rejected. I still had so much to learn.

As previously discussed, the book of Genesis tells us that because of a tree and man's choice, the whole world became cursed. Man's spirit in him, including yours and mine, was detached from its life source, Holy God, and caused everything to die. Also, in the book of Matthew, because of a tree, the cross, and Jesus's choice, we became righteous or made right with God. We were covered in sin, but now we walk in righteousness. We were once living by our flesh, but now we are led by the spirit. We were once covered by a robe of animal skin that has now been replaced and we are clothed with God's robe, a robe of royalty and love.

Our provision once came from the fields through sweat and toil and produced thorns, but because Jesus was beaten and bruised with a reed from the fields, He placed our provision upon His head, a crown of thorns.

We can receive freely from God the Father and now enter into His rest. God shed his own blood for our sins for all time. He chose to stay on the cross and give Himself up as a living sacrifice. Hebrews 12:2–3 (NIV) says, "For the joy set before him, he endured the cross, scorning its shame, and sat down at the right hand of the throne of God. Consider him who endured such opposition from sinners, so that you will not grow weary and lose heart."

Our freedom was the joy that He saw through the end of time that kept Him on the cross to die for us so that we might go free. And through that sacrifice, we are made righteous sons and daughters of God the Father. In addition to that, the letter to the Galatians 3:13 (NIV) says that Christ redeemed us from the curse of the law by becoming a curse for us, for it is written, "Cursed is everyone who is hung on a pole." We have been both redeemed and born again in the spirit. It is our minds, the centered self, that we must renew and train in this new knowledge and way of thinking as God is.

But I did not know all that back then. I thought God had rejected me because I'd done something to wipe it all away.

THE FOREIGN EXCHANGE

This strange confusion inside of me would not go away. Even though I was married to the love of my life and I was working hard to make a decent wage, I still felt lost. We were still in our young 20s and trying to make a go of things. However, things got worse. Rounds of layoffs soon began to find their way to both my wife's and my companies.

Many people were panicking as if they were all waiting for the final judgment of a trial hearing. According to my wife's account, her co-workers were in disarray, but not my wife and her optimistic, soft-spoken friend. They were just fine. They had an assuredness within them that things would work out. If not there where they worked, then somewhere else.

Well, sure enough, layoffs were in abundance, and my wife and her friend were two of the casualties. Workers were crying and worried about what to do next. They were filled with hopelessness and fear of the future. With the unemployment rate at about 7% according to the U.S. Bureau of Labor Statistics at the time,[27] people didn't know where they'd get their next job. However, my wife and her friend weren't concerned. Instead, they were the ones encouraging everyone else, even supervisors and executives above them. How were they able to do this? They were redeemed by the Lord.

What does it mean to be redeemed? The first man made us sinners and cursed us from birth, and no works of good could deliver us from this bondage and separation to make us right again or righteous. Jesus bought us back with his life, a ransom paid in full to darkness. Our spirit has been born again, made alive, opened, and reconnected back to God, revealing our higher self, our super nature. All of our sins, past, present, and future, have been canceled. We have been set free!

This is especially important to understand. More than understanding it, consider my stance on this topic. While the predominate Christian belief is that your salvation is secured, there are some who teach that you can somehow lose your freedom and the salvation that was already paid in full by Jesus if you do enough bad stuff. The Bible-teaching website, DB Ministries, uses Philippians 2:12 (NIV), "...continue to work out your salvation with fear and trembling," to argue that "if we are saved regardless of what we do, this scripture...would make no sense at all."[28]

---

27   Joanna Moy, "Recent trends in unemployment and the labor force, 10 countries," *Monthly Labor Review* (August 1985), https://www.bls.gov/opub/mlr/1985/08/art2full.pdf.

28   "Yes you can loose [sic] your salvation," DB Ministries, accessed August 9, 2021, http://www.dbministries.org/teaching/yes-you-can-loose-your-salvation/.

My question to this belief is the same question I asked in the previous chapter: If no amount of bad stuff has gotten you cursed and in darkness from birth and no amount of doing good could get you out of it, then how could you lose something you never could obtain or be qualified for in the first place? The answer is that you can't. Salvation is irrevocable. Therefore, believing that your connection with God can be lost is very dangerous and cannot be further from the truth. If you can lose your liberty and salvation through Jesus's redemptive work, then Jesus's sacrifice of His life was a temporary fix and not a permanent one. If this is true, then your salvation is up to you and dependent on your own actions, with judgment still looming over you. It would all be based on your performance, and would still be up to you to win or lose. By comparison, can your kids do anything bad that would make them no longer your children? No. You may not condone something bad they may have done or even choose to have no relationship with them, but their DNA still says they came from you! In the same way, we are sealed with God's DNA when we reconnect with Him, that is, when we reconnect with His divine nature attributes. So, your salvation can never be revoked! You are His and He will never give you up for anything or anyone, because He loves you with an unconditional love that no human can match nor has the capacity to adequately deliver. And He did this through our Lord and savior Jesus.

After my wife was released from her job, we went shopping. We bought her new business suits, shoes, and dresses. My thinking at the time was that if she invested in herself, she'd feel great, and people would take notice. We knew we would make it through this rough patch. To keep her focused and encouraged, I suggested she not watch the news or read headlines, because the job market was mostly discouraging. I asked her to not apply for openings she saw in the paper, because everyone else was probably looking at the same postings. I went on to suggest that she should decide what she really wanted to do and where she had a desire to work, rather than a place she felt she needed to apply to because they were hiring and we needed the income. She took my advice and ran with it. A month later, she had several offers from different employers. We chose one of them, and she was gainfully employed once again. It worked just like we had planned.

Later that week, I was let go from my job. I figured I'd take my own advice and approach it the same way. But it didn't go as planned for me like it had for her. I was out of work much longer than I expected, and the industry I was in was in far worse shape. Also, I was still haunted by the question of whether I was in right standing with God. It began to take its toll on me. I remember one night I was so emotionally low that nothing else really mattered that much to me anymore. I believed that I was doomed to live a life of mediocrity. After all, it was my destiny. I began to think that at some point my wife would eventually give up on me, realizing she had made a bad decision choosing me for a husband. All those encouraging words she used to tell me went silent in my head. I'll never forget those days because for the first time in my life, I felt hopeless. I never thought I would feel that way after going through so much growing up, but I did.

And with good reason, I thought. Why did I think I could be any different than where I came from? I had limited education, and even worse, God wasn't listening to me. I thought to myself that maybe I *was* too materialistic. I feared being poor so much that it consumed me, and God knew I wasn't really interested in what He was interested in: volunteering at church, going to all-night prayer meetings, or listening to boring gospel music. Perhaps that's why He had gone silent on me. I was defeated.

WHEN HE COMES TO YOU

That same evening, I heard a voice within myself say, *If you'll take one step, I'll take two.* Just like before when I heard that same voice speak within me about honoring my parents, I had no idea why it spoke to me or even what it meant.

You see, I was convinced I'd been found out: I was a fraud, a nice guy that people liked on the outside, but on the inside, God knew the truth. I was all talk with no substance. I had plenty of desire and aspiration about how life would be different for me, but no real plan for how to manifest it into reality. I had no purpose, I had no plan, and God knew it. Soon, my wife would know it, and everyone else would know, too. I went to bed that night with a heavy heart.

But that voice that spoke about taking a step wouldn't go away.

Once in bed, I felt as if I was drifting off a bit but knew I wasn't entirely asleep yet. I could hear the ceiling fan above us, and the AC unit coming on and shutting off. Then, in a corner of the bedroom, I saw a light. It was getting brighter as if something or someone was walking through the walls. I got out of bed and stood up. I stood on one side of the room and this approaching light was on the opposite side. It got brighter and brighter. It was so bright, it looked like daytime instead of night.

I looked around to see what was happening. Was I dreaming? No, I was awake. The light was very bright, and I was afraid to move.

Then, an audible voice spoke to me. I heard it not with my ears, but in my spirit. The light spoke to me in a very deep voice, called me by name, and said, "If you'll take one step, I'll take two!" As I was standing there, I was so afraid that I was trembling. But, for some reason, a calm welled up inside of me.

I looked down at my feet and lifted my right foot very slowly to take a step. As soon as I planted it on the floor, the light rushed to me like a strong wind and embraced me. My head was down looking at my feet on the floor, and I could see the brightness in front of me as I looked up a little; the brightness looked like a bright white garment.

He placed what felt like His hand over my head. I didn't look up, but I could feel it as the light shined brighter over me. He touched what felt like a single hair on my head. From that one hair, a powerful force of water or fire rushed through my entire being. It felt wet but it was dry. It sounded like a strong wind but flowed like a waterfall. It was freezing cold but hot as flames at the same time. And it ran through me from the top of my head to under the soles of my feet.

I began to see visions of the earth and galaxies, millions of them. I saw my wife and me sitting in what appeared to be the frame of a newly constructed building with people walking around wearing hardhats and carrying tools and cutting boards, working to put it together. Workers pointed at blueprints, and large trees surrounded the parameter. Then, I felt as if I was gently pushed back into our bed. My body was tingling on the inside from head to toes, flowing up and down inside of me. I was breathing heavy and trying to reason with what I had just experienced. I knew what dreaming felt like. This was something else.

I turned over to look at the clock. It read 3:34 a.m. on Friday, February 6, 1987. I tried to sleep for real this time, but I kept thinking about what just happened. A few minutes later, my wife tapped me on the shoulder.

"Are you OK?" she asked.

"Yes, I'm fine. Why?"

"You were just shaking and talking so much. It woke me up."

"I was talking? What was I saying?"

"I'm not sure exactly. It sounded like words from another language or something. You were talking pretty loud."

For the record, I don't speak, nor have I ever spoken, another language. I've always wanted to learn, but I never have. I explained to her all of what I was feeling the night before and what happened in this "dream" I had. After talking about it out loud to her, I began to ask myself, *Was this the experience I thought I was supposed to have when God accepted me?* I thought that it had to be.

At 4:45 a.m., I decided to call a church friend and see if he could explain it to me. To my surprise, he picked up the phone. I explained it all to him. He then told me to grab a Bible and turn to a certain passage, Jeremiah 20:9 (NIV), which reads, "But if I say, 'I will not mention his word or speak anymore in his name,' his word is in my heart like a fire, a fire shut up in my bones."

I looked at it and thought to myself, *So this must mean that I have been accepted.* After I hung up the phone, my wife asked me how I felt. I told her I felt great, and it was like a great weight was lifted off of me. I picked up a Bible and told her that for some reason I felt as if I understood the scriptures better. I couldn't explain it at the time, but I finally felt like I could read the Bible from beginning to end and I would understand it clearly.

As I was putting the Bible back on the nightstand, it slipped out of my hand and fell on the floor. As I reached down to pick it up, it fell open to this passage, Acts 2:2–4 (NIV): "Suddenly a sound like the blowing of a violent wind came from heaven and filled the whole house where they were sitting. They saw what seemed to be tongues of fire that separated and came to rest on each of them. All of them were filled with the Holy Spirit and began to speak in other tongues as the Spirit enabled them." I was perplexed as I read it, because I'd never read that scripture before, nor had I heard it preached, but it appeared to describe to me more accurately what I had just experienced, especially the part about the languages because that's the part my wife revealed to me, as I had no idea I was speaking.

At the time, we attended a church that didn't teach on those subjects. If they did, it was taught only as something that happened in the days of Jesus but was not for today, which is probably why my good church friend didn't mention it to me. But it was now my experience, an experience I remember so clearly that even as I'm writing about it now, I can feel it.

The next week, I received a call for an interview at a bank. I was given an offer that I accepted a few days later. I was working again, but this time as a different person.

WHY IT MATTERS

What I wasn't clear on before, I certainly understand now. I was literally overwhelmed and flooded with God's presence, His love, and His power by way of His divine self, the Holy Spirit.

The Holy Spirit is God. He is not an *it* or a divine influence. He is not a spiritual concept. He is a person or the personality of God in you. Like you, He has a will, intellect, and emotions. He is God with all the attributes of deity. He is the third person of the Trinity—equal with God the Father and God the Son. There is only one God, but He manifests Himself in three persons, whom we call the Trinity.

It's impossible to follow God and do the will of God unless the Spirit of God leads you. And the only way to be led by the Spirit is to follow God's command and be filled or controlled by the Spirit. This is why some who claim to know God through Jesus still live a defeated and powerless life—they haven't yielded their divine selves to God's spirit, which is real power. Interestingly, the Bible compares being filled with the Holy Spirit to being drunk. Someone who's drunk with alcohol is controlled and consumed by alcohol. Trust me, I've seen enough of that growing up to last me a lifetime. So, to compare, someone who is drunk in the Spirit is controlled and consumed by the Spirit. This is how God helps us live separated lives the way He intended by guiding us through our higher selves and not our lower selves. Ultimately, we are performing God's will on earth as it is in Heaven. No wonder liquor is sometimes referred to as spirits, because drinking too much will cause you to give up your conscious normal behavior to the alcohol, which can control you.

The inward power of His presence is the indwelling of the Holy Spirit. You know He's there because you sense an undeniable love, joy, peace, and assurance that wells up inside of you. Your spirit comes alive! That's the fruit, or the evidence, that you are a child of God and proof that you have been born again. You have been made new and aware of your higher self. Galatians 5:22–23 (NIV) says it like this: "The fruit of the Spirit is love, joy, peace, forbearance, kindness, goodness, faithfulness, gentleness, and self-control. Those who belong to Christ Jesus have crucified the flesh with its passions and desires. Since we live by the Spirit, let us keep in step with the Spirit."

His presence gives us the power and authority to forgive, to love unconditionally, to remember scripture, and to be made righteous and in right standing with God Himself. His presence comforts you, guides you, counsels you, talks to you, encourages you, and even tells you how to pray. He's the omnipresence of Jesus in your life and inside of you. Romans 8:16 (NIV) says, "The Spirit himself testifies with our spirit that we are God's children." It goes on to say, "In the same way, the Spirit helps us in our weakness. We do not know what we ought to pray for, but the Spirit himself intercedes for us through wordless groans. And he who searches our hearts knows the mind of the Spirit, because the Spirit intercedes for God's people in accordance with the will of God."

The best sampling of this manifestation is the documentation of the account of how the disciples received the indwelling of the Holy Spirit and what the purpose was of each visit.

The outpouring or the filling of the Holy Spirit is like being clothed with or submerged in his spirit. Galatians 3:27 (CEB) says, "...for all of you who were baptized into Christ have clothed yourselves with Christ." The power or the baptizing of the Holy Spirit is when He pours out on you. This is why believers are baptized by water. It's a ceremonial demonstration of being filled by God's spirit by being submerged in water. But it is symbolic of how the Holy Spirit clothes you when you are being filled by Him. It is this outpouring that gives you the ability to do the impossible, like healing the sick, raising the dead, casting out demons, making body parts regenerate, and moving financial and circumstantial mountains out of the way. It is not you or I who do these things, but God Himself by his spirit in you and on you. We do not have the capability or possess the supernatural power in this present body to do *anything* of God without His ability, except by way of the outpouring of His spirit *on* you.

Consider what Jesus said to his disciples in Acts 1:4–5 (NIV): "Do not leave Jerusalem, but wait for the gift my Father promised, which you have heard me speak about...in a few days you will be baptized with the Holy Spirit." He continued in verses seven and eight by saying, "It is not for you to know the times or dates the Father has set by his own authority. But you will receive power when the Holy Spirit comes *on* you; and you will be my witnesses..."

I, too, became a witness of this great, loving, and peaceful power He spoke of. No longer did I fear death, no longer did I feel as if I had no purpose or direction, and no longer did I feel that my family and I would be broke and poor.

If you're wondering if people who say they are saved but have not had the same experience as the apostles or I had are not God's children, that would not be accurate. They have been marked in their hearts, or possess the indwelling of His spirit, and because of this, they too have been made righteous. They have the power to love and are able to discern the word and hear God's voice. About that, the Bible says in Ephesians 3:16–17 (NIV), "I pray that out of his glorious riches he may strengthen you with power through his Spirit in your inner being, so that Christ may dwell in your hearts through faith."

So why do so many people claim to know God and live as if they don't? There are many reasons for that. Perhaps it's because they lack the knowledge or understanding of the need for the power of God's spirit guiding their lives. Some people who have been born again in their spirit have not renewed their soul or minds in understanding this new way of living because they are so used to living the old way with old thought patterns. Romans 12:2 says that we are to renew our minds and no longer follow the pattern of this world. The word "pattern" means to simply follow the form or model of something to imitate it. Without our thinking being renewed by God's word, we simply try and fit what the Bible says into our old way of thinking, which are distinct opposites of each other. Our spirits are renewed, but our minds are not. We have to learn God's way and be guided by His spirit to begin to understand and function the way we were originally intended to operate. When we do this, Romans 12:2 (NIV) goes on to say, "Then you will be able to test and approve what God's will is—his good, pleasing and perfect will."

Like being adopted into a new family, a family of royalty, there's a whole new way of life to learn. But old habits are hard to break. Consequently, and more accurately, we are no longer foreigners and strangers but fellow citizens with God's family and members of his household. We become a new citizen in a new country with a King who wants to be acknowledged as protector and provider and recognized as the Father. Though some believe they are in fact part of this kingdom family, they sometimes act as if they are still members of their old family, or old lower self.

If you have accepted Christ, then you are now an adopted son or daughter. You have been redeemed and sealed with God's spirit. Everything that He has is yours. No more sweating and toiling for things you need or desire out of desperation as if your life depends on it. You have been restored! Therefore, if any man be in Christ, he is a new creature, and old things are passed away; now all things have become new. You are no longer a slave to the curse and darkness; instead, you are God's own child. And since you are His, God has made you also an heir to all He possesses. In other words, you have been *legally* adopted and *legally* left an inheritance!

The forces of darkness do not want you to know this is available to you. Yes, there are benefits and wealth that people don't know they have: wealth from a royal inheritance that's legally and rightfully theirs, waiting for them to take hold of at any time.

But simply working hard is not going to get you a financial breakthrough. It's a spiritual matter, not a financial matter. And only by the power of being guided and filled by God's Spirit do enemy forces of darkness even take notice.

This is the only way to truly break free of the unseen bondages that hold you back financially. This is the root cause of why so many people on earth struggle to have an abundant life the way the Creator intended since the beginning. Though many try and break free with the greatest of efforts, and some appear to succeed, most don't—like Helen, like Doug, like my family after my parents divorced, like so many.

SECTION II: THE WAY IS CLEARED

CHAPTER 5

THE KINGDOM IN YOU

"The value of any experience is measured, of course, not by the amount of money, but the amount of development we get out of it."

—*Henry David Thoreau*[29]

You've probably heard testimonies of people who claim to have had near-death experiences. Many of the stories are similar: While declared clinically dead, they got a glimpse of the afterlife in a form of bright tunnels or welcoming family members who have passed. Some theorize it as paradise or nirvana. Beliefs range from Heaven being only a state of consciousness to Heaven being a physical location where their soul and spirit go on to live and experience life with others forever and ever.

In the last chapter, I stated that you are one with Jesus and sealed with His spirit when you have accepted Him as the way to all freedom. With it, He becomes your king, and you are now an heir or royal of His kingdom, that is, a person who has the legal right to receive the property of someone who dies or a person who has the right to become a king or queen to claim a title when the person holding it dies. That's the actual definition of the word heir. In

29   Henry David Thoreau, *The Writings Of Henry David Thoreau: Journal, ed. By B. Torrey. 1837-1846. 1850-Nov. 3. 1861* (Charleston, SC: Nabu Press, 2012).

this section, we explore what and where this kingdom is, the benefits of being a citizen of it, your inheritance as an heir, and how to manifest the benefits into your life today.

Jesus referenced the kingdom as a place He came from and the place He was going back to once the work that He was sent to earth to do was completed. Many people claim to have died, gone there, and come back to life here on earth. They speak of their experiences in Heaven and what they've witnessed by describing its atmosphere firsthand. They explain the sights and sounds of it and how peaceful the experience was, with no fear but with unconditional love instead.

STORIES FROM THE OTHER SIDE

One such story was chronicled in detail by a neurosurgeon, Eben Alexander, who died and came back to this earth's consciousness in 2012. It was so compelling it made the cover of *Newsweek* magazine.[30] From this experience, he went on to write a best-selling book called *Proof of Heaven*. In his *Newsweek* article, he expressed that, as a neurosurgeon, he did not believe in the phenomenon of near-death experiences because he grew up in the world of science. Since his father was a neurosurgeon, he wanted to follow in his footsteps. He theorized that science gave pretty reasonable explanations for what happened in a person's brain and how it functioned when people faced a near-death experience. With that in mind, he drew comfort in that belief until he was faced with a near-death experience of his own.

In 2008, he was lying in a coma for seven days. He described how he heard a message during that time, saying to him, "You have nothing to fear. There is nothing you can do wrong."[31] He went on to explain that while his body was in a coma, his mind and inner self were alive and well. Not only that, he said that someone was with him, a companion of sorts in this different state. He felt no fear but only unconditional love. What a fascinating account!

Reading about what happened to him while lying on that table in a coma and the way he described the mouthless conversations and the "hotter than fire

---

30   Eben Alexander, "Proof of Heaven: A Doctor's Experience With the Afterlife," Newsweek, October 8, 2012, https://www.newsweek.com/proof-heaven-doctors-experience-afterlife-65327.

31   Ibid.

and wetter than water"[32] explanation of his thoughts reminds me of what my experience was like in my bedroom in February 1987. I can also remember that sense of unconditional love and peace he described.

While I was moved by what he depicted, I didn't want to settle on simply one person's claims of what he had experienced in the afterlife, so I went on to research other accounts of near-death experiences as a means of comparison. I found thousands. The Near-Death Experience Research Foundation (NDERF.org) collects stories from *people* all over the world who *have seen* the *other side*.[33] Eben Alexander's story was listed there, too. The following paragraphs give short descriptions of others I read.

"THE MOST GLORIOUS FEELING"

In 1994, an orthopedic surgeon described how, while talking to his mom on a payphone during a trip, a sudden blue flash of light came out of nowhere. He later felt his body fly backward and then forward. Next, he described how he could see his own body lying on the ground. He thought he was dead, but said he felt no grief or ecstasy. He later described how he began to drift away, seeing his kids playing at home, and said to himself that they'd be OK.[34] In an interview with the *New Yorker*, he said he was "…surrounded by a bluish-white light" and "…an enormous feeling of well-being and peace" came over him.[35] He continued saying how the highest and lowest points of his life raced by him—with a perception of accelerating and being drawn up. He recalled saying within himself that during that state of consciousness it was the most glorious feeling he had ever had, and then—slam! He was back in his body.

"IT WAS REALLY BRIGHT"

Another case I read was about a woman who had two chronic, life-threatening digestive disorders at age four. By age eight, she was ready to give up until

---

32   Ibid.

33   "Near-Death Experience Research Foundation," NDERF, accessed August 17, 2021, https://www.nderf.org.

34   Oliver Sacks, "A Bolt From the Blue," the *New Yorker*, July 16, 2007, https://www.newyorker.com/magazine/2007/07/23/a-bolt-from-the-blue.

35   Ibid.

something unexplainable happened. She was sitting on a tree branch 30 feet in the air when it cracked. She fell down into a hollow at the base of the tree, where she was trapped for six hours. She says she died and went to Heaven: "It was really bright, and I sat on Jesus's lap, and He told me, 'Whenever the firefighters get you out, there will be nothing wrong with you,'" she told *TODAY*, "and I asked Him if I could stay and He said, 'No, I have plans you need to fulfill on earth that you cannot fulfill in heaven.'"[36] When she woke up, her illness had healed. Her mom authored the book *Miracles from Heaven*, which was later turned into a film.[37]

"I FELT NOTHING BUT PEACE AND HAPPINESS"

About 20 years ago, an orthopedic surgeon described how she almost drowned while kayaking in Chile, and her heart stopped for more than half an hour. "Soon after leaving my body, I was greeted by a group of beings who were simultaneously familiar and unfamiliar. This may sound strange, but I felt nothing but peace and happiness in their company," she wrote on mindbodygreen.com. "When I was separated from my physical body, I was simultaneously aware of what was happening in Heaven and what was unfolding on the riverbank where I had drowned. I thought about my husband and my children, my parents and siblings (and not at all about my work or other earthly worries)."[38] She went on to author the book *7 Lessons from Heaven*.[39]

I bring these accounts of Heaven from what people have said they witnessed because there are still some who hold a more agnostic point of view to life, meaning that while Heaven seems like a glorious place to go to after you die, there is still uncertainty here on earth.

---

36   Lindsay Sobel Dyner and Chris Serico, " 'I crossed over': Survivors of near-death experiences share 'afterlife' stories," TODAY, April 3, 2015, https://www.today.com/health/i-crossed-over-survivors-near-death-experiences-share-afterlife-stories-t12841.

37   Ibid.

38   Mary C. Neal, "I'm A Doctor Who Had A Near-Death Experience. Here's What I Saw on the Other Side," mindbodygreen, updated May 13, 2020, https://www.mindbodygreen.com/articles/what-i-learned-about-heaven-from-a-near-death-experience.

39   Mary C. Neal, *7 Lessons from Heaven: How Dying Taught Me to Live a Joy-Filled Life* (New York, NY: Convergent Books, 2017).

There's no denying that life can be heartbreaking at times. I've had my share of struggles. I can see why Heaven is so appealing, and based on these few experiences we've just read, who wouldn't want that kind of peace and unconditional love? Jesus said in John 16:33 (AMPC), "In the world, you have tribulation and trials and distress and frustration; but be of good cheer [take courage; be confident, certain, undaunted]! For I have overcome the world [I have deprived it of power to harm you and have conquered it for you]." Jesus is King, the King of the entire universe! He came to the earth to reestablish the Father's kingdom, which was the original intent from the very beginning when He created mankind. The instruction to man, in the beginning, was to be fruitful, to be productive, multiply, and re-create after your kind to create a population and society, to subdue the earth, to rule or conquer, and bring it into subjection along with everything in it, including the serpent.

However, man was not instructed to rule over each other. This mandate has not changed. Unfortunately, man's natural tendency to rule has spun out of control. This is what happens when we function by the lower nature and it's in control and not connected to its source, which is God himself. You may ask, "Why is there so much death, destruction, poverty, and hunger?" My reply is that man's soul and fleshly power of greed and survival have gone completely untethered, and the desire to rule and satisfy himself has no bounds. As I've illustrated previously, this was not God's intent.

Regardless, God does not go back on what He started. Instead, He circumvents the problem by introducing a new strategy that was in place long before creation ever began. This strategy involves man empowered by God's spirit to subdue the earth with the power of God through the Holy Spirit in man to reconnect himself once again in a relationship, like parent and child, and provide his every need for continuing His mandate from the beginning, that is, to make earth like Heaven. And He's left you and me a great and abundant inheritance to ensure that we accomplish our mandate and purpose while on this earth, should we choose to accept the mission.

HEAVEN IN YOU

First, Heaven is inside of you. Ephesians 2:6 (AMPC) says, "He [God] raised us up together with Him [Jesus] and made us sit down together [giving us joint seating with Him] in the heavenly sphere [by virtue of our being] in Christ Jesus [the Messiah, the Anointed One]." Seated in the heavenly realm by virtue of our being, that is, our spirit. We have access to Heaven 24 hours a day by virtue of our spirit.

Imagine you are in a distant country away from family and friends. While they can't see you, nor can you see them, there is a way to connect again, a way where you can see where they are and their surroundings and they, in turn, can see where you are in that other country. This can be accomplished, of course, by our smartphones through FaceTime. With this technology, not only can we see each other from different parts of the world at the same time, but we can also acquire what we see from each place if we choose to. If by FaceTime, you showed a friend something at a local market you wanted to buy them that you thought would be a nice gift and they told you to get it for them, in a matter of days by way of shipping, you could have in your possession the same item you saw from across the world. Connecting with Heaven through your spirit works the same way. Whatever is needed for you here on earth, Heaven has it available for you 24/7. So, when a need arises, you can access it from there and bring it here, by virtue of your spirit, through your soul, and eventually into this physical three-dimensional realm.

This is such a simple concept to grab hold of, yet the religious mind—that is, the mind that tells you to follow certain rules, abstain from what the world has, and be satisfied with what you have—will say that this is a gross misinterpretation of the text. Let's go further. Jesus talked quite a bit about not worrying about the things you need in this world. Your father knows you need them, He went on to say. He said don't try and store treasures or material wealth here on earth so that you are always supplied for when you need or desire anything. Instead, store it in Heaven. Matthew 6:19–20 (AMPC) reads, "Do not gather and heap up and store up for yourselves **treasures on earth**, where moth and rust and worm consume and destroy, and where thieves break through and steal. But gather and heap up and **store for yourselves treasures in heaven**, where neither moth nor rust nor worm consume and destroy, and where thieves do not break through and steal; For **where your treasure is, there will your heart be also**." Treasures are things. More specifically, they are things that you value or place value on. If they were not things, then He would not have referenced rusting, decaying, and something being stolen or destroyed. He said to store up and value the things in Heaven, that is, the *things* that are laid up for you only. These things are protected and are always available when you need them. For where your heart or spirit is, there is also where your treasure, or what you place value on, is.

When you look to Heaven for your supply and not the way the world goes about seeking supply, then you are seeking the original or abundant supply that does not run out from the one who freely gives. Let's continue.

Verses 22 through 24 (AMPC) say, "The eye is the lamp of the body. So if your eye is sound, your entire body will be full of light. But if your eye is unsound, your whole body will be full of darkness. If then the very light in you [your conscience] is darkened, how dense is that darkness! No one can serve two masters; for either he will hate the one and love the other, or he will stand by and be devoted to the one and despise and be against the other. You cannot serve God and mammon [deceitful riches, money, possessions, or whatever you trust in]."

In short, if you are seeking provision by your natural-based, five-senses nature, your lower consciousness, then you are going about it by way of the darkness, which is the old cursed way. Therefore, you are responsible for everything that comes with it, because you are serving the thing rather than the thing serving you. He also says because of this, your conscience is darkened, meaning you become blind to the higher self, that is, your spiritual guidance, and continue to walk or be guided by earthly, logical, and emotional means, which is usually the slow, sweating, and toiling way.

He goes on to say in verses 25 and 30 of Matthew 6 (AMPC), "Therefore, I tell you, stop being perpetually uneasy [anxious and worried] about your life, what you shall eat or what you shall drink; or about your body, what you shall put on. Is not life greater [in quality] than food, and the body [far above and more excellent] than clothing? But if God so clothes the grass of the field, which today is alive and green and tomorrow is tossed into the furnace, will He not much more surely clothe you, Oh you of little faith?" Once again, He's referring to things. Worry, anxiousness, desperation, and scheming to provide for yourself are not concerns of the higher self.

Every example you read earlier of those who experienced death and came back to life expressed how peaceful, majestic, free, and timeless they felt as they experienced this higher self of divine reality and awareness. This is what we are suppose to experience here on earth when we live and are led by our spirit and not just by our souls and body. When you are guided and living by your spirit, you experience more peace within you and have a better outlook of circumstances and people around you, *without fear.* You have an assurance that whatever you need will work itself out when you believe it will—because it will.

The Bible describes Heaven this way in Revelation 21:21 (CEB): "The twelve gates were twelve pearls; each one of the gates was made from a single pearl. And the city's main street was pure gold, as transparent as glass." Revelation 21:18 (CEB) reads, "The wall was built of jasper, and the city was pure gold, like glass." John 14:2 (CEB) says, "My Father's house has room to spare. If that weren't the case, would I have told you that I'm going to prepare a place for you?" Revelation 22:1–2 (CEB) says, "Then the angel showed me the river of life-giving water, shining like crystal, flowing from the throne of God and the Lamb through the middle of the city's main street. On each side of the river is the tree of life, which produces twelve crops of fruit, bearing its fruit each month. The tree's leaves are for the healing of the nations…"

Rooms, leaves, fruit, streets, walls, gold, pearls, jasper, and rivers. We can identify with all these things and comprehend them because they are also here on earth. It's just a difference in location. To give an example for context, if I told you I had something very valuable and life-changing for you, and I wanted to give it to you but it's in another country, would you say, "Oh, well, it was a nice gesture but there's nothing I could do to get it"? Or would you say, "No big deal. What country? I'll find a way to bring it to me or go there and get it myself!"? The questions for some people would probably be, "Do I trust the person who says they have this thing they want to give me?" and "How much would it cost me to try and get it?"

These are the same questions people ask themselves about anything they wish to obtain beyond their normal experiences, especially if it's to be given to them. This dark place we live in has trained us to naturally question and be skeptical about *anything* we hear of that can be positively life-changing for us, especially if we can't earn it. Don't misunderstand me because I get it. Part of the reason in my opinion, is because people in general can be selfish or look for ways to deceive others. After all, even from birth, it's not uncommon to see a growing child not want to share or scream that something is theirs. Our own life's disappointments, other people's experiences of letdowns, what we've been told growing up, and sayings we've adopted as truth like, ("If it sounds too good to be true, then it probably is" or "Be careful what you wish for because you just may get it") cause us to be skeptical of anything we perceive as *too good*. But why should someone be careful about what they've desired or wished for? Isn't that the whole concept of hope?

To some, good things always seem to have a catch to them, so to appear smart and practical, they believe that it shows good judgment to be cautious or skeptical. I've had a career in sales so I've experienced it firsthand. I even hear friends say, "I wouldn't ever want to be rich—too many problems," as if to say that being poor is easier or comes with better problems? These are all-natural negative traits, behavior, and thought patterns that develop over time when operating and conducting life employing the soul and flesh in a cursed system that's designed to work against you.

However, when trusting the spirit, the higher self, peace, and conviction of your divine conscience will guide you and help you navigate your decision-making process successfully. This way, even if something that doesn't make sense is presented to you, your spirit will guide you because you are promised peace that comes from the mind and heart of Christ, who promises to guide you in all truth. Look at 1 Corinthians 2:16 (AMPC): "For who has known or understood the mind [the counsels and purposes] of the Lord so as to guide and instruct Him and give Him knowledge? But **we have the mind of Christ** [the Messiah] and do hold the thoughts [feelings and purposes] of His heart." God cares about what you care about; therefore, He's very interested in helping you get to where you want to go.

ROYAL BENEFITS OF CITIZENSHIP

Because of Jesus, we can be royal sons and daughters of the highest God, our Father. His spirit can be in communion with our spirit, operating as one when we yield to Him. The story of the prodigal son, or the one who has returned, says it best.

Luke 15:17–22 (NIV) reads, "When he came to his senses, he said, 'How many of my father's hired servants have food to spare, and here I am starving to death! I will set out and go back to my father and say to him: Father, I have sinned against heaven and against you. I am no longer worthy to be called your son; make me like one of your hired servants.' So, he got up and went to his father.

"But while he was still a long way off, his father saw him and was filled with compassion for him; he ran to his son, threw his arms around him and kissed him. The son said to him, 'Father, I have sinned against heaven and against you. I am no longer worthy to be called your son.' But the father said to his servants, 'Quick! Bring the best robe and put it on him. Put a ring on his finger and sandals on his feet.'"

This story is such a wonderful picture of how God sees us and, unfortunately, how we sometimes see ourselves. When we think the worst of ourselves, God always thinks the best of us, because He sees us as we are, which is like Him, not as we were. Like the signet ring that was given to the young son to identify what family he belonged to had a seal on it, for us, the seal is in our hearts, God seals us with the Holy Spirit to show who we belong to. The son's lack of shoes would traditionally signify to strangers that he was a slave and had ownership of nothing. But since he was not a slave, his father said "… quickly put sandals on his feet and a robe on him." In the same way, we are no longer slaves to this present world, and we should always wear the robes of the higher self, like royalty. Also like royalty, we have been given the entire estate as our own.

The Bible says that Jesus did not come into the world to condemn it but to save it by sacrificing Himself for it and establishing a new system of government and the original plan for your life. Like any system of government, its citizens have rights and privileges. We quote this during the Christmas holidays, but I don't think many people focus on the "government" part. Isaiah 9:6 (NIV) says, "For to us a child is born, to us a son is given, and the government will be on his shoulders. And he will be called Wonderful Counselor,

Mighty God, Everlasting Father, Prince of Peace." What *government* will be on His shoulders? Heaven's government!

The definition of a government is; the political direction and control exercised over the actions of the members, citizens, or inhabitants of communities, societies, and states; a branch or service of the supreme authority of a state or nation, taken as representing the whole. God Himself through Jesus came to establish His government of righteousness or right way of living, called the Kingdom of God, as the model or pattern for man to follow through the guidance of His spirit on this earth. But only to those who believe. These *believers* are God's citizens of the kingdom.

Jesus did not come to merely govern a country or a state, but he came to govern the whole world! Jesus is king, and we are the people or citizens of Heaven that will implement His system and demonstrate love, peace, and abundance of wealth through His process for our lives. Jesus is our example of how the Kingdom of God operates, and we are to duplicate these righteous ways on earth as kingdom citizens, producing abundance for ourselves to help spread God's great compassion for mankind through our generosity. Since this is His mandate for us, then how can we be generous if we have nothing or very little to offer or be generous with, except our attitude and expressions of compassion? Offering thoughts and prayers is admirable, but in today's toxic religious and political climate, it has become a punchline to many people when they hear it said or expressed. Real people with real problems want real and tangible evidence of Heaven's abundance from those who supposedly represent it. Prayer that doesn't lead to concrete action toward our family, friends, and community is a fruitless and incomplete prayer. Prayer and action must always be profoundly united. Results must be demonstrated and shown—especially when economic provisions are at the forefront of most people's worries and concerns.

Jesus said this in Luke 4:18–19 (NIV): "The Spirit of the Lord is on me, because he has anointed me to proclaim **good news to the poor**. He has sent me to proclaim freedom for the prisoners and recovery of sight for the blind, to set the oppressed free, to proclaim the year of the Lord's favor." What does "good news to the poor" mean? I believe it means just what it says! The good news to someone poor is that they will be abundantly supplied for economically, their lack has been addressed, and they will be poor no more!

Did Jesus address poverty while He was on the earth? Of course, He did. Now, I'm aware of those people who claim that Jesus was referring to being poor spiritually, not economically. If this was true, does the passage also mean that He was referring to setting people free who were spiritually blind, spiritually in prison, and spiritually oppressed? Some would argue, yes, that's exactly what He was referring to. Let's take a closer look and see if that's what He did.

Luke 7:20–22 (AMPC) reads, "So the men came to Jesus and said, 'John the Baptist sent us to You to ask, are You the One Who is to come, or shall we [continue to] look for another?' In that very hour, Jesus was healing many [people] of **sicknesses** and **distressing bodily plagues** and evil spirits, and to many who were **blind**, He gave a free, gracious, joy-giving **gift of sight**. So, He replied to them, 'Go and tell John what you have **seen and heard**: the blind receive their sight, the lame walk, the lepers are cleansed, the deaf hear, the dead are raised up, and the poor have the good news [the gospel] preached to them.'" Certain words are in bold to emphasize the fact that He was not referring to anything spiritual except when He addressed evil spirits. Physically blind eyes were given visual sight, physically diseased people with leprosy were given cleansing of their skin and were rid of the bodily disease, physically deaf people were given actual hearing in their ears, and physically dead bodies were being raised back to physical life or resurrected and walked out of physical graves. Likewise, Jesus wouldn't allow physically manifested deliverances for everyone else, but tell the poor that they had to just be encouraged and wait until death to experience the good life in Heaven. Jesus spoke to them and gave them good news too, meaning **the way to profit** and obtain provision and abundant supply for themselves here on the earth! And for you and me, if you are a kingdom citizen, this same divine wealth is already yours and available now. Your treasures are stored in Heaven, available and ready for whenever you need or desire them, 24/7!

Religious thinking and dark influences do not want you to know this or understand it. If you do, you'll want to claim your inheritance and begin to advance God's mandate and kingdom agenda on this earth with a righteous heart, thereby denouncing and canceling the works of evil and darkness at work in your life. Keeping you blind with images of religious churches begging for money is a demonic tactic with imagery to match. Unfortunately, it's very effective. God's people struggling to meet budgets, using car washes and bake sales, dues and building funds, crooked evangelists, and false teachers are all evil influential tactics designed to occupy your thinking so that you are not supposed to want or desire material wealth. These tactics are meant to show how the church should be an example of living a minimalistic life successfully.

On the other hand, there are churches and other nonprofit organizations that desire to truly represent Heaven in a way where God's goodness is on display by feeding the hungry, clothing and housing those who are less fortunate, and encouraging the souls of the disenfranchised and brokenhearted. How are they to do this without abundant supply? What does it say to the world when churches are struggling financially and appear to come across as begging when they are simply asking for support? When I see this, I begin to feel as if a part of the gospel message is missing. The message of hope and provision from an abundant and resourceful God doesn't appear to match the required mission.

Don't get what I'm saying confused—evangelism in its purest form is not something we can buy. In its most effective form, evangelism happens when one person lovingly brings the good news of God in Christ to another, which should be the desire of every believer. That is evangelism, and it doesn't cost any money. But some people are uncomfortable in sharing their faith and feel that sharing the gospel is a very private matter. With that in mind, churches help fill this void through wide evangelism, through modes like radio, television, the internet, and missionary outreach. The church that I attend, Lakewood Church in Houston, is active in this way and makes a huge impact for the gospel and the kingdom locally in our surrounding communities and worldwide in other communities. We are always conducting some form of outreach: holding blood drives and food drives, providing shelter, supporting local food banks, sending out missionaries, and providing healthcare services in other countries where access or cost is prohibitive. These efforts help doubters and unbelievers witness the gospel being demonstrated.

As for those who are struggling financially, doesn't the gospel address those issues and concerns also? What would happen to someone's faith if you paid off their mortgage, or bought them a car, or financed their business, or cleared their student debt? I believe, at the very least, it would open their hearts to hearing what you have to say, and perhaps they would become more receptive after seeing your selfless generosity being demonstrated in such a dramatic way.

2 Corinthians 8:9 (AMPC) says, "For you are becoming progressively acquainted with and recognizing more strongly and clearly the grace of our Lord Jesus Christ [His kindness, His gracious generosity, His undeserved favor, and spiritual blessing], that though He was [so very] rich, yet for your sakes He became [so very] poor, in order that by His poverty you might become enriched [abundantly supplied]."

Some opponents call this the *health and wealth* gospel. They say it's a gospel that's built on greed and materialism. Additionally, as I've been told by many, this passage does not mean financially poor but spiritually poor. But I don't believe that. I believe it means exactly what you've just read—financially and economically poor. If Jesus was *spiritually* poor, he could *not* have performed such wonderous and great physical manifestations, or miracles. Instead more accurately, this passage compares where He came from, Heaven, to where He was, Earth. His earthly supply was like living in poverty compared to Heaven's abundant supply. Besides, poor people are not spiritually poor, they are economically poor. This is why it says that through His *poverty* you might become enriched. The word "poverty" means; the state of one who lacks a usual or socially acceptable amount of money or material possessions. By saying Jesus was in poverty is to say He did not depend on this world's provision for supply, like getting a job. He trusted in the wealth of Heaven for His supply. He operated by and through divine order, from His higher self not His base nature, though he was human like everyone else.

Abundance means different things to different people, regardless of the amount. And while most everyone is working hard to provide for themselves and their families, I can't imagine many of us would mind if we were given a little extra boost in the areas of supply. The very reasons why people work, seek overtime on their jobs, take on extra work, play the lottery, gamble, or accept government stimulus checks for both businesses and personal purposes are to soften the blow of constantly working for provision, in hopes that a little extra will give them some breathing room between work and leisure. We are not created to simply work our whole lives without a means of appreciating and enjoying the fruits of that work. The true nature of who we are does not want to work hard just to get by for a day and do it all over again. It's the God in us that says something is not quite right about this way of living.

Yet, there are still those who believe that wealth and abundance are evil and should be avoided at all costs. If money and wealth are so destructive and corrupt and could destroy mankind, then why is wealth so hard to obtain for most of the population? My reply is that it's *not designed to destroy us*! Only someone void of compassion for those who go without basic needs or supply every day would imply such an evil juxtaposition. It's also a feeble representation of a mighty and compassionate God who says He loves you and will provide for you. The truth is, He has. Psalms 37:3–4 (AMPC) says, "Trust [lean on, rely on, and be confident] in the Lord and do good; so, shall you dwell in the land and feed surely on His faithfulness, and truly you shall be fed. Delight yourself also in the Lord, and He will give you the desires and secret petitions of your heart."

YOUR EARTHLY INHERITANCE

God made an oath that He would restore His relationship with man through a man, and He searched for that person by examining every man's heart. The Bible says He found such a person in Abraham. God made a covenant or an agreement with him that would eventually filter through and to all the nations of the world. Galatians 3:16 (AMPC) reads, "Now the promises [covenants, agreements] were decreed *and* made to Abraham and his Seed [his offspring, his heir]. He [God] does not say, 'And to seeds [descendants, heirs],' as if referring to many persons, but 'And to your Seed [your descendant, your heir],' obviously referring to one individual, Who is [none other than] Christ [the Messiah]."

It goes on to say in Galatians 3:26–29 (AMPC), "For in Christ Jesus you are all sons of God through faith. For as many [of you] as were baptized into Christ [into a spiritual union and communion with Christ, the Anointed

One, the Messiah] have put on [clothed yourselves with] Christ. There is [now no distinction] neither Jew nor Greek, there is neither slave nor free, there is not male and female; for you are all one in Christ Jesus. And if you belong to Christ [are in Him who is Abraham's seed], then you are Abraham's offspring and [spiritual] heirs according to promise."

Who was Abraham, what are spiritual heirs, and what was promised? According to the biblical account, Abram, which means "the Father [or God] Is Exalted," is later named Abraham, the Father of Many Nations, a native of Ur in Mesopotamia, and is called by God to leave his own country and people and journey to an undesignated land where he will become the founder of a new nation. He obeys the call and (at 75 years of age) proceeds with his barren wife, Sarai, later named Sarah ("Princess"), his nephew Lot, and other companions to the land of Canaan (between Syria and Egypt). There the childless septuagenarian receives repeated promises and a covenant from God that his seed will inherit the land and become a numerous nation.

God promised him, saying this in the book of Genesis 12:1–3 (AMP): "Now [in Haran] the Lord had said to Abram, 'Go away from your country, and from your relatives and from your father's house, to the land which I will show you; and I will make you a great nation, and I will bless you [abundantly], And make your name great [exalted, distinguished]; And you shall be a blessing [a source of great good to others]…and in you all the families [nations] of the earth will be blessed.'" In the next chapter, Genesis 13:1–2 says, "So Abram went up from Egypt to the Negev, with his wife and everything he had….Abram had become **very wealthy in livestock and in silver and gold.**"

So, here we see the blessing of Abraham who became financially and physically wealthy with livestock, silver, and gold, not spiritually wealthy. Why did God do that for him? He did it to show that if you are rejoined to him through the finished work of Jesus, then these same manifested promises are for you also. Again, *if you belong to Christ, then you are Abraham's offspring and [spiritual] heirs according to God's promise.*

CHAPTER 6

GLOBAL MISSION IMPACT

"A life is not important except in the impact it has on other lives."
—Jackie Robinson[40]

Living in Texas certainly has its benefits. It's a very large state with plenty of wide-open spaces. It has several major cities with every modern convenience imaginable, and the weather is relatively warm for most of the year, with its share of rain and sometimes snow. Further south in Houston, not far from the Gulf of Mexico where I'm from, we get our share of tropical storms, tornadoes, and hurricanes. Just by living here, we become astute with weather forecasts and terminology, just like meteorologists do. It's just one of our norms for living here. We gain an understanding of the six main components of weather: temperature, atmospheric pressure, wind, humidity, precipitation, and cloudiness.[41] Together, these describe the weather at any given time. These changing components, along with the knowledge of atmospheric processes, help meteorologists study the weather and forecast what the weather will be.

---

40   Irwin B. Bergman, *Jackie Robinson* (Chelsea Juniors, 1994).

41   "Weather," National Geographic, accessed August 9, 2021, https://www.nationalgeographic.org/encyclopedia/weather/.

With severe thunderstorms that last too long comes major flooding in different parts of the city. And when high-pressure systems meet low-pressure systems, we get tornadoes and hurricanes. When this happens, it becomes major news. You may remember some of the names of certain tropical cyclones and hurricanes that became famous because of what they did to Houston and the surrounding areas: Alicia in 1983, Allison in 2001, Rita in 2005, Ike in 2008, and Harvey in 2017. I've witnessed the property damage and loss of lives firsthand.

The storm's effects don't end when it has passed, though. The rebuilding and reconstruction of neighborhoods, communities, and businesses, and the emotional toll of it all, linger for quite a while—for months and even years. Through all of them, my extended family and I have never had our homes flooded or experienced any major loss of life, income, or property. Sure, we've had our share of big trees broken around us, but never anything significant.

In February 2021, we encountered and survived an extreme cold snap that ravished thousands of communities and left them without electrical power or running water for days. Icy roads and snow everywhere we looked was a new one for Texans. Throw in an ongoing world pandemic and not everyone was going to make it out alive. Many did, but, unfortunately, a lot of people didn't.

I'm not bringing up these devastating events because they are fond memories. Instead, I'm touching on them because of the responses of people I saw helping other people in times of crisis. I witnessed firsthand people sharing whatever they had to help someone in need they didn't even know. Food, clothing, shelter, transportation, survival gear, and whatever it took were provided when loving people responded simply because they thought more about others than themselves.

Houston is a very diverse city. During times like those, race, political preference, religion, gender, nationality, none of it matters. It's just about people helping people. More than that, it's about sharing resources from those with more than enough with those with less. My family saw these special acts of kindness on full display in our own backyard.

During the time of Hurricane Harvey, the home we lived in was on a one-acre lot with beautiful pine trees in the front and back parts of our yard. Right outside of the neighborhood, we saw the caravan of people in vehicles coming from the Galveston area stuck in traffic for hours and days trying to escape the pending storm scheduled to slam the area once touching land. My kids and I took bottles of water and handed them to whomever we could in the middle of the highway, not thinking how these small random acts of kindness would come back to us in a big way.

When the storm finally rolled over us, it uprooted and knocked down a huge tree in our backyard. It fell perfectly in the only place it could that didn't hit the house or the detached garage. The trunk of the tree was about 4 feet in diameter, and its length was about 20 yards. It broke in half on the way down, so the top part of the tree fell over our back fence where our yard backed up to a ravine. As my wife and I were looking at the fallen tree, we both wondered how in the world we were going to remove this thing. City workers were tied up responding to power outages, flood areas, and debris left in the streets within 50 square miles. We knew we would not hear from them for at least 10 days. We certainly didn't have the tools to remove it ourselves, so this was a big dilemma for us. Quicker than we could analyze the situation, a solution drove into our driveway and then entered our backyard. It was a large caravan of neighbors riding four-wheelers, supplied with chain saws, buckets, bags, and leaf blowers descending on us like superheroes. Within 17 minutes or so, that tree was chopped into small pieces, bagged, and stacked at the end of our driveway ready for the sanitation department to pick up when they got back to a regular schedule. We were shocked! When they were done, we asked how much we should pay them. They saluted us and quickly moved on to the next house that needed help. We stood there utterly amazed and stunned, but humbled and grateful. This was a Class A example of people with the resources and the means helping people without—what a concept!

In almost every human tragedy involving other humans, some wish to harm others, leaving victims in the aftermath. There are heroes and villains, the fortunate and the less fortunate, and, of course, the haves and the have-nots. By design, we are all called or summoned to be the best version of ourselves through our words (what we say) and our deeds (what we do). We try and teach our children to always be considerate of others and compassionate when the opportunity arises to do so. When we do this, we exemplify the love of who we are on the inside of us, the God part of us. Furthermore, we are demonstrating the love He has for all of us through our actions. The privileges that our Father has given us, we freely give to someone else. Since we have been given, we freely give (by word, deed, or both) to everyone and anyone who will receive. This is the epitaph of what Jesus commanded, in John 14:21 (AMPC): "Whoever [really] loves Me will be loved by My Father, and I [too] will love him and will show [reveal, manifest] Myself to him [I will let myself be clearly seen by him and make myself real to him]."

Every person who loves and has transformed their minds to the understanding of the higher self or is in lockstep with God's Holy Spirit is automatically called to the entire world with a mandate to shine that light of love against the kingdom of darkness and break its rule over others. That's our mission, our call, and our purpose. The passage Matthew 5:14–16 (NIV) says, "You are the light of the world. A town built on a hill cannot be hidden. Neither do people light a lamp and put it under a bowl. Instead, they put it on its stand, and it gives light to everyone in the house. In the same way, let your light shine before others, that they may see your good deeds and glorify your Father in heaven." In chapter 1, I described one of the characteristics of God: He is light. Therefore, we are light, too, and we must shine this light on others through our words and deeds. There is no better way to let our light shine than through our generosity of sharing. Therefore, it's important that we are prosperous in every way so that we can extend our light in sharing throughout the world without having a thought or concern about our own provision.

With this love we have, we *must* shine light in every capacity of our lives, starting with the sphere of influence we have already been given. This circle of influence we have is for our self-growth and is our training ground for ultimately spreading the light to every capacity of society, demonstrating compassion and oneness with our Creator. The first man and woman were instructed to till the ground in the Garden of Eden until paradise was to spread throughout the earth. This mandate has not changed. It involves taking back what the darkness has stolen and restoring society to its former glory in knowing and walking in our true divine self, pointing to God the Creator of All as our guidance, source, provider, and truth.

DO YOU KNOW YOUR PURPOSE?

Look at a day in the life of Jesus as He walked and lived on this planet. Matthew 9:36–38 (AMP) says, "When He saw the crowds, He was moved with compassion *and* pity for them, because they were dispirited and distressed, like sheep without a shepherd. Then He said to His disciples, 'The harvest is [indeed] plentiful, but the workers are few. So pray to the Lord of the harvest to send out workers into His harvest.'" This is just one day in His life, yet still, He went about His days walking in compassion, amongst large crowds, understanding the people were helpless in correcting their own lives, issues, and dilemmas without knowing who they really were and what power they naturally possessed. So, He empowered the ones He was teaching to become agents of change and light amongst darkness to course-correct what was rightfully theirs from the beginning. The passage goes on to say how in the next chapter, Mathew 10:1 (AMP), "And Jesus summoned to Him His twelve disciples and **gave them power and authority** over unclean spirits, to drive them out, and to cure all kinds of disease and all kinds of weakness and infirmity." Jesus gave them power, and, in turn, they used it to do what Jesus did. It is only by divine power that you and I can dispel the root cause of sickness, disease, and poverty that can impact a society. And Jesus gives it to anyone who seeks Him. But before attempting to touch the world, you must first determine the part of society you are destined to influence, starting with where you currently are.

I've created five influences, or pillars, of the world's system that impact society. (Some refer to these as mountains of society.) They include the areas of financial, legal, entertainment, social, and health, which represent what we need to function in this earthly five-senses realm. The chart below shows some of the subsegments for each function within the categorized pillars.

FINANCIAL	LEGAL	ENTERTAINMENT	SOCIAL	HEALTH
TAXES	GOVERNMENT	SPORTS	FAMILY	MEDICAL
WORK	JUDICIAL	HOBBIES	FRIENDS	FOOD
INCOME	LAWS	MEDIA/MOVIES/TV	COMMUNITY	PHARMACY
INVESTMENTS	PENALTIES	MUSIC	CO-WORKERS	MENTAL

These pillars impact your center (soul) and base (physical) nature. To accentuate this point, take the first letter of each represented pillar in order to spell out the word FLESH—all pillars of society allow you a capacity to perform and operate for provisions that satisfy and replenish your physical self, or the flesh. God has placed you in and gifted you with one of these sections of society to positively impact life for yourself and others.

It's a training ground for you to develop in the areas you will need to fulfill your purpose on earth. More specifically, it shows how to be guided by the higher self within you, for discipline, so that when you arrive at your rightful place in life, you are mature enough to handle it. This way, you become an example of what living right or operating by original design looks like to those who are simply living a life based on survival or the lower self. Whether you are taking orders at a fast-food restaurant, sweeping floors at a school, caring for the elderly at a nursing home, or being a stay-at-home parent, everything you are involved in has already been put in place for you to get what you need en route to your destiny.

Your life should look like, sound like, and act as the divine nature of your Creator here on earth. Romans 12:2 (AMPC) says, "Do not be conformed to this world [this age], [fashioned after and adapted to its external, superficial customs], but be transformed [changed] by the [entire] renewal of your mind [by its new ideals and its new attitude], so that you may prove [for yourselves] what is the good and acceptable and perfect will of God, even the thing which is good and acceptable and perfect [in His sight for you]." Conduct your life from a standpoint of intentional originality, that is, be yourself from your higher self. Don't simply play a role where you are trying to fit. *Being your true self is enough.* Don't be some imitation of what others want you to be or even someone you are trying to be like. Be authentic and be honest before God. Doing this will unlock the truth within you. Once discovered, dare to be led by truth and act on it. Then you will discover the power to produce and experience the true wealth that has been inside of you since the day you were born.

THE FAMILY BUSINESS

I was once was a business development director of an international recruiting firm operating out of two offices, one in Sacramento, California, and the other in a small city in the valley further south called Stockton. We helped outside employers fill roles for IT (information technology) and accounting professionals within their organization, matching employees with certain skill sets to what employers were looking for in the marketplace but could not find. In essence, we represented both the employer and the potential employee as a mediator to marry the two for a successful career relationship.

I always found it interesting to hear from one side, say the employer, about the ideal candidate they were looking for. In most cases, the skills, personality, and salary rate the employer was looking for rarely existed, which is why they would opt for having a recruiting firm search for them. As for the candidates, it was a matter of matching the skills correctly, but most lacked interviewing and soft skills. They were knowledgeable about the software, code language, or whatever technical skills the role required but didn't spend a lot of time developing interpersonal skills.

To land the right role for both the hiring client and the prospecting job seeker, we had to get both sides to give up a little to make it fit. Sometimes it was a matter of getting the employer to raise the pay levels of an offer or ask the candidate to come down on their salary expectations. Regardless, it took a delicate balancing act to make it work. Our team was very successful at it.

What sticks out to me most about that job was when the candidates' spouses would call and thank me for getting their husband or wife that dream role or just getting them working. For the most part, it wasn't because the candidate had all the skills that the employer was looking for. Sometimes the hiring employers would say a candidate can have all the skills and experience required for the role, but if they appeared to come off as a jerk or a prima donna, they wouldn't hire them. That's because having someone who can blend in with synergy and teamwork with the rest of the employees meant more to them than bringing a certain set of skills but with a bad attitude. This made it easier for me to select candidates, because I knew what the employers' core motivations were, something that I'd never see listed on a job posting or qualifications requisition.

Even better, sometimes it was easier to get the employer to talk to our candidate. They trusted that we had a relationship with them, so however we described them beforehand, pros and cons, they were more at ease because they knew what to expect. This is one of the benefits of having a mediator, someone who knows both sides of the matter so that they can speak on each other's behalf.

Imagine if God was the employer, and He was looking for a certain role to fill and He calls you in for an interview. Would you be nervous? Would you try and say the right words based on what you thought He'd want to hear? Or would you simply be yourself, even based on what God already knows about you? This may sound like a silly example, but the reality is that God is hiring! And He's looking for people who are comfortable enough just being who they are and are not afraid to become what they are destined to be. He knows everything about you, warts and all, yet none of that matters to Him. He loves you just the way you are and has accepted you long before you were ever created. Can you accept Him for who He is? Can you even accept yourself?

So often, I find people with such low self-images of who they believe they are, because they equate who they are with what they've done or failed to do. The good news is that when I was a mediator for candidates who thought they could never qualify for a career job at a major company because of their lack of *whatever*, they still landed the role because they had an insider, me. For those of us who identify ourselves as followers of Jesus, He is that mediator for us in all things. He's the insider you need to know for what would otherwise be impossible for you to carry out without having the proper timing, knowledge, experience, connections, or background to make what you want to happen on your own. 1 Timothy 2:5 (NIV) says, "For there is one God and one mediator between God and mankind, the man Christ Jesus." Since he is the mediator between you and God, lean on Him, tell Him your heart's desires. Don't think about what others might think or say; let God show you your purpose, and don't waste another day of this precious life He's given you not doing what you have been designed to do. You could never be fulfilled otherwise. Don't be afraid of what you might hear. If you know the message was from God, go for it. He has promised to provide everything you'll ever need to accomplish what He's created you for.

I've been on both sides of the job-hunting equation—I've been the candidate looking for a job and I've been the employer looking for a candidate. As a candidate, you bring one thing with you, your resume. As an employer, you must have several things to offer to entice and convince the right talent to come and work for you and not the competition. Often employers need something more than just a salary, like a benefits package. While the salary may satisfy your need for buying things for you and your family to live a certain way of life, the benefits packages are the extras provided to keep you healthy and continuing to come back to work again and again, such as medical, dental, vision, retirement funding, stock options, bonuses, company vehicles, etc. If the role requires you to travel from state to state or to another country, the employer provides whatever you need to accomplish the task at hand effectively and efficiently.

God is no different. He understands what you'll need to live out your destiny and function at optimal capacity. Not only does God pay well, but He has also promised added benefits. Whatever you do for God, He wants you representing the business well because you are a reflection of Him. Therefore, there is *nothing* that God would hold back from you when you are about His business. Look at what is said about it in these few passages:

Jeremiah 29:11–13 (NIV): "'For I know the plans I have for you,' declares the Lord, '**plans to prosper you** and not to harm you, plans to give you hope and a future. Then you will call on me and come and pray to me, and I will listen to you. You will seek me and find me when you seek me with all your heart.'"

Ephesians 3:20 (AMPC): "Now to Him Who, by [in consequence of] the [action of His] power that is at work within us, is able to [carry out His purpose and] do **superabundantly, far over and above all** that we [dare] ask or think [infinitely beyond our highest prayers, desires, thoughts, hopes, or dreams]."

2 Peter 1:3–4 (NIV): "His divine power has given us **everything we need** for a godly life through our knowledge of him who called us by his own glory and goodness. Through these he has given us his very **great and precious promises**, so that through them you may **participate in the divine nature**."

For some people, to be about God's business means to be a part of a church ministry of some sort or to preach the gospel as a pastor, evangelist, or minister. Not all people are summoned to the calling of structural ministry. During some of my experiences in conversations with people about sharing their faith or topics concerning God, Jesus, or the gospel, their first thought is that I must be referring to church involvement. On the contrary, you are to shine your light wherever you are. Whether you're in the financial, legal, entertainment, social, or health services of society, do your best for God, and He will make your name great as He promised your forefather, Abraham.

CHAPTER 7

WEALTH AND MONEY

What we really want to do is what we are really meant to do. When we do what we are meant to do, money comes to us, doors open for us, we feel useful, and the work we do feels like play to us.

—Julia Cameron[42]

I've mentioned a time or two how we weren't brimming with money when I was in my teen years. It wasn't always that way, though. When my mom and dad were together, we did not want for anything, at least from what I could tell. We had late-modeled vehicles, as children we had what we wanted for Christmas, and there was never a time we went hungry.

My dad was a good man who many admired, not without his faults, but a noble man whom I also admired. So much so, that I wanted to emulate him as a husband and father one day when I had my own family. He had a wonderful sense of humor and made us laugh. But he also didn't mind expressing himself when he got angry. He was a tireless worker with discipline, and he demanded excellence from us when he gave us a task. When he felt he knew something, no one was going to convince him or change his mind about what he thought

42 Julia Cameron, *The Artist's Way: A Spiritual Path to Higher Creativity* (New York, NY: TeacherPerigee, 2016).

he knew. Perhaps it was his military background or maybe he just saw enough mediocrity around him that he was determined not to be that way himself. I'm only speculating because he never shared his thoughts on those matters. I just observed and listened to him talk and watched him in action. I admired him. After all, he was my dad, and I was proud to be his son.

From a child's perspective, we were living in a middle-class neighborhood. I didn't know how he was paying for everything. All I knew was that he worked as a diesel mechanic at a big trucking company and my mom was at home with us. As I looked around at our way of life and compared it to others I knew from school, we were doing better than some but probably not as good as others, which is likely how most people were living. There were times, though, when I would analyze my surroundings and ask myself, "How am I going to be able to afford all this when I get older and have my own family?" I didn't know much about money or finances. My parents never really taught or shared a lot of that stuff with us. The secrets to obtaining and building wealth were not family discussions. So, from what we could see as children, you were to get a job, get a paycheck, and buy things. While I knew in my heart there was more to gain in life than what I saw from my childhood experiences, that's pretty much what everyone else did: got an education, found a job, and bought stuff. My older brother did it, his friends did it, and all the neighbors' moms and dads were doing it.

Keep in mind that in the 1970s and early 1980s, there was no public internet or world wide web. The public could access information through the library, almanacs, the yellow pages, the white pages, television, and radio. In short, my parents never taught us about finances, and in our schools, those subjects were reserved for higher learning institutions. I'm not making excuses, but you just don't know what you don't know.

Most people today are a culmination of what they have experienced and what they were exposed to. Using my own upbringing as an example, in my neighborhood I was surrounded by families who appeared to make decent wages for the way of life they chose to live, including my own family. Had not the devastation of divorce impacted us the way it did economically, I probably would have aspired for the same type of lifestyle. Similarly, if a person had grown up in a poor nation where everyone had huts and were slaves and it seemed like a normal thing, then that person would have a higher probability of becoming a product of those experiences as an adult. However, if a person's life experiences as a child were going through private or boarding schools and being raised with maids and butlers doing the undesirable tasks around their home, luxury would be their normal. Chances of them producing the same for their families and the next generation are just as high as their children doing the same.

Like kind produces like kind. It's a law of nature and why in the U.S. we are so fascinated, interested, and intrigued by rags-to-riches stories. Mainly, it's because of the breaking away from the norms of what should happen to someone depending on where they started in life. It's not normal for people who started life economically poor to finish their lives in the top percentile of the nation economically, and each generation's likelihood of out earning their parents is decreasing.[43] But we love it when it happens for someone. Most believe that if it happened for someone else, then it can happen for them, too.

However, their journey of success is *their* journey, and your path to wealth is *your* journey. Neither can be duplicated exactly. The connections, good breaks, and timely circumstances that may have assisted them along the way to their successful destination will not be duplicated the same way for yours. Even a subtle nuance of something going slightly differently will alter your path, taking you to an entirely different outcome. Pyramid schemes and multilevel marketing (MLM) are built on this philosophy, which is why so many people fail at them. Of course, most people who try MLM schemes are undeterred by this, which is why most go from program to program in hopes that *this* time with this *new* product will produce a different outcome. Trust me on this one. I know a lot of these people, and not one of them is financially better off than when they began nor are they still in the same program they started with for more than one year. None of them I know has produced what they thought they would, based on the testimonies from those at the top of the pyramid. Some talk like they have, but they have very little to prove it.

---

43   Marcus Lu, "Is the American Dream over? Here's what the data says," World Economic Forum, September 2, 2020, https://www.weforum.org/agenda/2020/09/social-mobility-upwards-decline-usa-us-america-economics/.

For this reason, we should aspire to be wealthy, not rich, as our goal in life. Some people consider rich and wealthy as the same thing, but they are technically different. Let's look at both and compare.

WHAT IT MEANS TO BE RICH

In simple terms, being rich is having the ability to spend lavishly due to a high income or sizable financial windfall. To be rich means you are involved with the making and spending of the money. No matter the income source, it will always involve your efforts to produce it. Like an actor, a sports star, or a CEO of some major corporation, you must be present and involved to generate the amount of money your efforts can bring. Furthermore, a rich person is usually looking for ways to make more money and more ways to keep it from being spent, with the end goal of trying to keep or hoard as much as possible for safekeeping. Even if that person owns certain expensive items like a Rolls-Royce or a Ferrari, they will seldom drive it because of the exuberant costs of maintaining the item to keep it, not to mention the insurance and regular upkeep. In short, this is what defines someone rich, someone with a lot of money and few assets, which is why so many rich people hardly ever retire because, quite frankly, some can't. They must continue working just to keep the money coming in. This is mostly a fear-based motivation. They know once it's gone, it's gone.

Think of this same mindset, but instead for those who are not rich. A survey, conducted in early April 2020 on an online platform called KnowledgePanel,[44] found that groups of Americans who were financially vulnerable before the onset of the pandemic are now feeling a disproportionate burden. Fluctuating economic predictions and a volatile employment landscape have created significant financial stressors. Many of those surveyed are in desperate need of help. They've been laid off, their businesses have shut down, or they're struggling to stay afloat financially. For a lot of people, a job or what they can produce from their efforts is what they will depend on for financial security.

---

44   "Report on the Economic Well-Being of U.S. Households in 2002 – May 2021," Federal Reserve, updated May 25, 2021, https://www.federalreserve.gov/publications/2021-economic-well-being-of-us-households-in-2020-executive-summary.htm.

The bottom line is that even being rich can be a form of slavery. It's a much higher form of it, but it's still slavery. In other words, you *must* perform to keep what you have and what you want to produce coming in. I once had a billionaire tell me, "Most people can't be a billionaire. You want to know why? Because for most, having millions is enough."

WHAT IT MEANS TO BE WEALTHY

Wealth, on the other hand, is owning considerable assets that provide long-term prosperity. For example, if someone owns a home that has a considerable amount of equity against the mortgage they carry, let's say $500,000, then that home is definitely an asset, even though it has a loan with a pay balance against it.

Most wealthy people I know have the attitude that it's only money and that they have the means to get more of it when they need or want it. They treat money more as a resource or a means to producing something greater in mind, like ingredients in an extravagant meal or the parts necessary for a project they're building. Finding a few million here and there to achieve what they want to get done is not considered an obstacle or a problem. They simply find the resource needed and continue with the vision of the project, because they understand the money is inconsequential. It's only a part of what's needed to manifest the vision in mind.

Most people would go into cardiac arrest just by the questions and the what-ifs! I find that the wealthy do not live in the fear of outliving their money, but the rich often do hold that financial fear. This is what separates the rich—they have money and hold it as a god of protection that they have to slave for and try to hoard as much as possible. Then there are the wealthy, who know it isn't a god, but a tool to be used for their desires and more. This should make more sense to you when the Bible says in Matthew 6:24 (AMPC), "No one can serve two masters; for either he will hate the one and love the other, or he will stand by and be devoted to the one and despise and be against the other. You cannot serve God and mammon [deceitful riches, money, possessions, or whatever is trusted in]." When people put their entire trust in money, they usually have no need or desire for God to supply for them, because they believe they have all they need in money.

Money has its place. It is neither moral nor immoral. Instead, money is amoral. It is only good or bad depending on whose hand possesses it. For balance, understand that God wants you to be wealthy. He wants you to be wealthy more than you want to have wealth! He just doesn't want the wealth to have you, meaning that there should be nothing in your life that you are holding on to so tightly that you can't give it up if you need to. Therefore, the law of giving will be important to your wealth building, which we will cover in the next chapter. It's the principles of giving that are the big keys to your financial and prosperous future. If you find that you are having trouble releasing something that you possess, then that thing possesses you. You don't possess it. In essence, its value means more to you than the value of your relationship with God. Hence, God says that you can't serve both. Who do you trust for your life and provision, the thing or God? I will detail exactly how and why this law of giving works so well in the upcoming section.

WHAT IS MONEY?

The basic definition of money is anything that is commonly accepted by a group of people in exchange for goods, services, or resources. Every country has its own exchange system of coins and paper money. The Bible records the first bartering exchange taking place by the first man and woman's children. Genesis 4:1–4 (NIV) says, "Adam made love to his wife Eve, and she became pregnant and gave birth to Cain. She said, 'With the help of the Lord I have brought forth a man.' Later, she gave birth to his brother Abel. Now Abel kept flocks, and Cain worked the soil. In the course of time Cain brought some of the fruits of the soil as an offering to the Lord. And Abel also brought an offering—fat portions from some of the firstborn of his flock."

Cain and Abel learned about offering from their parents. Adam and Eve learned the need to do an offering to the Lord from God Himself or angels. There was no one else on the planet to teach them. Keep in mind, God had already given man rule and dominion over the earth; He did not take it away when man turned away or disconnected himself from God. Man had full authority to do what he chose with the authority and dominion that was given to him. Unfortunately, man gave away his position to the ruler of darkness, and the earth became cursed. As for man's provision, it became up to him to provide for himself and his family. God essentially had been kicked out and His hands were tied, so to speak, because He gave rule to man and He could not go back on His word. Man chose disobedience over God, and he did it of his own free will. God was still there; He did not abandon Adam and Eve. But if they wanted God's help or intervention in times of need, they had to invite God in and give Him something sacrificially of their own volition—something to offer in exchange for what God would provide for them. In other words, they bartered.

God will not take something from you nor give something to you forcefully. It must be of your free will. Through your own will, you can choose to give what belongs to you back to God. By doing so, it gives Him legal rights and power to do whatever He chooses with what has been given to Him. If you know the nature of God, then you know He is a giver. Therefore, when He gives back to you, it comes back multiplied and in abundance.

As believers, we have willingly given our entire lives to God; therefore, God has the legal authority to do as He pleases with our lives because we are His children, and we trust Him—well, some of us anyway. But even so, our soul and free will are still under our control and operation. Oftentimes, we want God to help us, but we sometimes want that help under our conditions—it must be done when or how we want it to be done. Furthermore, we only want help with the things we can't seem to handle, not the things we think we can handle on our own. This does not sound like the agreement that we made when we say we've offered our lives to God. To me, it sounds conditional rather than unconditional.

If you've ever wondered why so many Christians don't live by the guidance of their higher selves, it is because they are not renewed in their souls. Their spirits are perfect and they are a new creature in Christ, but their souls are still a work in progress, as it is a choice to accept what God says and begin to train their thinking to the understanding and operation of their God-like selves. Perhaps this is why so many do not experience the abundance supply in their lives that has been promised as an heir of Abraham. They won't trust God with *everything*, especially when it comes to money.

I believe after the fall of what man and woman experienced, they saw a *big* difference in how things were before the curse and then what life was like after the curse. I'm sure once they realized the next day that they must now produce for themselves, they started to understand the magnitude of how far they had fallen and what life would be like without God's guidance. I'm pretty sure if it was me, I'd cry out day and night asking how I could turn this state of living around. Of course, God did not abandon them. He was still with them, but not in His full presence, interacting with them like before. Instead, He operated only in spirit apart from them, and the entire Old Testament revealed how that turned out for everyone after them.

Back to the topic of money. While money today has replaced bartering for goods, the principles of producing money or wealth still apply. Your ability to provide for yourself and your family comes from a few factors working together. First, you need your health, ideas, and skills. Without these for yourself, you'll have to depend on someone else's. Next, you'll need to use your God-given gifts to stand out from the crowd. If everyone had the same gifts, there would be no distinction. Next are the available resources you'll need—you must have some level of knowledge or ability, and creativity also helps. Even with all that, you must put forth some effort to make all this work towards a common goal. In exchange for a portion of all those things combined, let's say a few hours a day, you'll get money so that you can provide for yourself and your family. Essentially, money is inside of you, and the more **h**ealth, **i**deas, **s**kills, **g**ifts, **r**esources, **a**bility, **c**reativity, and **e**ffort you're willing to showcase, the more money you can create. All these things are in everyone, because God provided them for us in advance before we were even born. It's called HIS GRACE.

Look at what was told to the early Israelites after they were set free from Egyptian rule and slavery, as found in Deuteronomy 8:17–18 (NIV): "You may say to yourself, 'My power and the strength of our hands have produced this wealth for me.' But remember the Lord your God, for it is he who gives you **the ability to produce wealth**, and so confirms his covenant, which he swore to your ancestors, as it is today." So, it's God who gives to us, inside of us, through HIS GRACE to produce wealth, and that's how we create money. If you choose to, you can honor Him again by giving back to Him the grace

He's freely given, not because it is commanded of us but because we choose to. In return, He promises to *always* provide for us with more of whatever we need or desire and whenever we need it—in abundance.

HEAVEN'S CURRENCY

Earlier in chapter 5, I said that Jesus came to establish Heaven's mandate on earth and that this mandate comes from the Kingdom of God, which is Heaven's governmental system or order. A strong government of a nation provides for its citizens with its protection and laws. A government also produces its country's currency. There are currently 180 recognized currencies across the world.[45] The British pound is thought to be the world's oldest currency that's still in use, its origins dating back to the eighth century.[46] In general and in no specific order, the U.S. dollar (USD), the Canadian dollar (CAD), the euro (EUR), the British pound (GBP), the Swiss franc (CHF), the New Zealand dollar (NZD), the Australian dollar (AUD), the Japanese yen (JPY), and the South African rand (ZAR) round out the list of top tradable currencies.[47] Well, Heaven has a trading system, too, with its own currency. It's called faith.

We have all been given a measure of Heaven's currency to use in any way we choose. The difference between God's currency and earthly currency is that God's currency has universal appeal, and it spends anywhere and everywhere. The exchange rate offers a very high yield on its rate of returns! This is how we begin to operate like God when we tap into our faith and depend on the laws of the divine, which have already been in place since before time began, for a return on our investment of faith.

I've used this passage of scripture before but it's worth repeating and expanding on. 2 Peter 1:4 (NIV) says, "Through these, he has given us his very great and precious promises, so that through them you may participate in the

---

45   "List Of Currencies Of The World – Updated 2021," Flags World, accessed August 10, 2021, https://flagsworld.org/world-currencies.html.

46   Ed Lowther, "A short history of the pound," BBC, February 14, 2014, https://www.bbc.com/news/uk-politics-26169070.

47   "List Of Currencies Of The World."

divine nature...." Promises are like the laws of the divine—they are in place and are immovable and irrevocable.

To impact society in a great and positive way, you must be committed to a cause and be willing to be a solution for that cause, which is why you must understand your calling and what you are called to do. Chances are good that whatever path your heart is gravitating towards, or you have a solution you wished existed to a problem, this indicates that you may be the one who should create and provide the answers. Unfortunately, most people don't step out into their convictions because of a lack of time and money. It's this fear of lack of provisions without knowing where they will come from or the source you can turn to that can be paralyzing for a lot of people. And God knows this. Therefore, he has supplied you with everything you'll need beforehand, and it's stored up for you to withdraw from whenever you need it by faith. If you understand the abundance you have in the Kingdom, you are not worried about hoarding up the provision on earth because you know you have an unlimited supply in Heaven! This is how we can be generous to others freely, which is also the very definition of being wealthy.

Through the world's system of supply, sweat, toil, and earning just enough on a paycheck, you can never reach your full potential in life because you are limited in so many ways. For example, you limit yourself whenever your habits of living exceed your paycheck in some form or another. You could scale back and live within your means, but you can't forecast setbacks and losses because they usually come at inconvenient times and without warning. If a paycheck is all you depend on, then you'll work harder to find more money, which is just a distraction wrapped in making a living. This way of living will ultimately keep you from reaching and discovering the power stored up in your true divine self or understanding your full potential in God, thereby simply conforming to and becoming content with just having enough for this month's bills.

Making more money by getting an additional source of income that involves your efforts or trying to save up enough for the future can be a lifelong distraction. Your desire to do things that are more meaningful and filled with a deeper purpose becomes stronger within, but it can become hard to pull away because the way of living needs the paycheck. Look, I know you have to work.

Working is God's will. But there's a distinct difference between working simply for a paycheck and working for a purpose that speaks to your entire being. Until you are free from the constant demands of making a living, you can never fulfill your purpose—and that's not living! Jesus said in John 10:9–10 (AMP), "I am the Door; anyone who enters through Me will be saved [and will live forever], and will go in and out [freely], and find pasture [spiritual security]. The thief comes only in order to steal and kill and destroy. I came that they may have *and* enjoy life, and have it in abundance [to the full, till it overflows]." This *life* he's referring to is also the life of purpose, freedom, and abundance—freedom in every way. That's true wealth.

Imagine if your every need were met without debt. What would you do with your life? This is hard to imagine for most Americans because they can't see themselves as free financially. To even attempt to manifest this idea into their lives, they do it the only way they know how—scale back drastically and live on a budget. Listen, budgeting has its place. If you know you're undisciplined when it comes to finances and you also know you're an impulsive buyer, then, yes, you need to buckle down, assess your heart, and get to the root of what's causing you to be so impulsive and spend money so carelessly.

Beyond that, there is no power in budgeting or living so tightly that you can't enjoy even the little things your work is providing for you. There is a reason why most people don't take their financial advice from a homeless person— they offer no proof in their own life for the advice they share. That's not to say that they weren't some financial genius before this part of their life took a turn, because we don't know someone's story about how they've gotten where they are and we should always be sensitive to anyone who is struggling with whatever it may be. But some claims require proof, and if being homeless is the result of this advice, then it may not be worth following. (In fairness, I'm sure they can probably tell you what *not* to do with money.)

One of the biggest lies ever told to the people of God is that they should not desire nice things in abundance. They reason that those nice things are of the corrupt world, and we are not of the world. To a degree, this theology has merit. But the proper context is not that you can't have things; you just mustn't let the things have you! The scripture in 1 John 2:15–16 (NIV) says, "Do not love the world or anything in the world. If anyone loves the world, love for the Father is not in them. For everything in the world—the lust of the flesh, the lust of the eyes, and the pride of life—comes not from the Father but from the world."

How do you know when things have you? When you *love* them. The scripture clearly states that you should not love anything in the world. This is idol worship. If you find yourself stressing or worrying about not having enough of a certain thing or the loss of it, then you are in love with something that cannot fulfill you or love you back. If you are willing to do whatever it takes to obtain something, get rich or die trying as someone suggested, and you sacrifice your peace, joy, and contentment in the process, then you are in love with things. You are serving the lower base nature and starving your super nature.

ACCESS BY FAITH

As we begin to understand more that the Kingdom of God is the government of God and his believers are its citizens, then it should not be a stretch to understand that this government provides just like any other. The United States of America is one of the world's superpowers. We are one of the top five wealthiest countries on earth, according to NASDAQ.[48] Yet, there are still citizens here who have not taken advantage of all the resources this country provides, and, in some cases, this country has not provided adequately for some of its citizens. Even our military veterans who have given their lives to protect our freedoms and way of life go without in this country as a civilian.

A strong country's strength is its citizens. During the Olympics on the world's athletic stage, each nation wants to put forth their best athletes available to compete and display the country's pride and strength against other nations. God is no different. He wants His nation, the Kingdom of Heaven nation, to represent Heaven well, which is why he would repeatedly say to the early nation of God in Ezekiel 36:28, "….you will be my people, and I will be your God."

The currency of God's kingdom is faith. Everyone has faith. Like muscles or money, it's up to you to exercise your faith and make it grow to do unimag-

---

48   Prableen Bajpai, "World's 5 Richest Nations by GDP Per Capita," NASDAQ, May 20, 2021, https://www.nasdaq.com/articles/worlds-5-richest-nations-by-gdp-per-capita-2021-05-20.

inable things on earth for the Kingdom of Heaven. Just like there are different kinds of currency for different countries, faith is the currency of the Kingdom of God and it is the only acceptable way you gain access to the kingdom. You've probably heard the saying, "Money is power." Faith is no different, but it is far more powerful than money. Faith moves things that money can't. Money can't love you or heal you when medical practices have come to the end of their studies. Money can't make a lost loved one come home. Money can't erase years of hurt and pain from sexual abuse. Money can't be a father or a mother. Money can't get you into Heaven's gates, but faith can. By faith is how you receive *everything* from God: "For we live by faith, not by sight."

WHAT IS FAITH?

Hebrews 11:1–3 (NIV) says, "Now faith is confidence in what we hope for and assurance about what we do not see. This is what the ancients were commended for. By faith, we understand that the universe was formed at God's command, so that what is seen was not made out of what was visible." So, faith is what we use to manifest what we desire out of Heaven and into earth. If you look up the word "faith" in the Merriam-Webster dictionary, it defines it like this:

FAITH (noun)

1: allegiance to duty or a person: LOYALTY.

2: belief and trust in and loyalty to God.

3: something that is believed especially with strong conviction.[49]

First, it describes faith as a noun. We've learned in school that a noun is a person, place, or thing. Therefore, faith is *something*. The scripture in Hebrews describes it as a *substance*. These two initial observations suggest that the substance, a noun, is something that can be seen—not something that's seen by the natural eyes of the senses, but by the eyes of your spirit, your supernatural senses. To effectively use faith in the divine realm, it must first be acquired by what you can see in your spirit before it can be manifested and seen by the natural eye. Next, we see that it is something that requires trust, loyalty, and

---

49   "faith," Merriam-Webster, accessed August 9, 2021, https://www.merriam-webster.com/dictionary/faith.

conviction to get it to do whatever it is supposed to do for you. When you be-lieve something to be factual, you act on it. If you see a chair and have a desire to sit down, for example, I can't imagine you'll ponder as to whether the chair will allow you to sit without falling over or the chair breaking. You recognize that it is a chair, you've sat in one before and so have others, so the decision to sit when you see one is not a struggle of thought at all. You have total and complete trust that when you sit on it, it will do exactly as you believed it to do. In fact, you would be shocked or surprised if it didn't.

Now let's compare how we use faith to the way we use money. The U.S. dollar is not a concept. It's a thing. It's a promissory note made of paper that is backed by the government of the United States. A promissory note is a financial instrument that contains a written promise by one party (the note's issuer or maker) to pay another party (the note's payee) a definite sum of money, either on-demand or at a specified future date. Even if the money is transferred digitally, the numbers on the screen represent actual money, which you can choose to convert into physical cash. You don't need to think much about the regulatory process of exchange from the vendor to the U.S. government's treasury. If the bills are not counterfeit, you have total trust that when you give the seller the bills for the items, you get in exchange what you have desired to purchase and receive. We do this every day and without much thought. Faith works the same way, in that faith is the currency of the divine realm and is backed by Heaven's government, the Kingdom of God, and re-turned in exchange for what you have imagined it to be here in the physical realm. All of this takes place inside of you.

An example of a faith transaction manifesting itself in the earth realm is Val-entine's Day. You decide that you want to express your appreciation to the one you love on that very day. You think to yourself, *What would be a nice gift of expression to show how much I love this person?* As you think about the things they like and the things they would want, you land on an idea in your mind. You can see it: 24 red and white roses in a marble vase. You then decide to search online for the picture you've created in your mind. You see it on RedandWhiteRoses.com (not an actual website). You select the item, pay the asking price and delivery fees with a debit or credit card, and have it delivered directly to your soulmate's home or office for that specific Valentine's Day.

When it's received, they love you for it—mission accomplished. All this was done with a thought, a desire, and an action. Did you doubt the roses existed? Were you concerned at all that the money you paid was enough? Were you nervous about them being delivered? If you answered no to any of these, then that's how faith works. Once you can think of what it is you desire, can see it inside of your spirit, and take the necessary actions to make it happen, it becomes reality by manifestation in the earthly realm. Faith causes thoughts to become things. Everything on the earth was first *thought* before it became a thing. However, divine manifestation starts with speaking the thing you see in your spirit into reality with confidence that you *will* have what you say.

Scripture says in 2 Corinthians 1:20 (AMP), "For as many as are the promises of God, in Christ they are [all answered] 'Yes.' So, through Him we say our 'Amen' to the glory of God." What God has promised is *always* yes. He has no need to say no to His own promises, as some might assume. By applying your amen to it, in affirmation to His truth, you can have what it is you ask of Him. You have no need to wonder if God will say no, because He simply doesn't say no to His own word. If He said it, then put your confidence in what He has said and it will be yours.

CHAPTER 8

YOU HAVE DIVINE AUTHORITY

"Where there is power and where it flourishes, there it is and there it remains because God has ordained it."

—*Martin Luther*[50]

My mother had a reputation of being a woman who spoke her mind and feared no one. Don't get me wrong—she was a very giving person and wouldn't turn away anyone if they were in need. But when it came to doing things she needed to get done or to bothering one of her children, you would be in for a fight if you got in her way. Whether she comprehended or not was inconsequential to her. Remember that she only had a sixth-grade education, so she trusted people with whom she had relationships and trusted her good ole survival gut instincts. For the most part, this worked out well for her. She didn't care whether she understood you or the point you were trying to make; all she cared about was that you understood her and the points she was trying to make. Believe me when I tell you, as children, we did not want my mom to have to intervene in a situation. Chances were pretty high that it was not

---

50   Martin Luther, *Commentary on Romans* (Grand Rapids, MI: Kregel Publications, 2003).

going to go well, and it would be that week's topic of conversation by friends and neighbors.

When money was short, and that was most of the time, she was very resourceful. She was not as astute as others when it came to numbers and calculations, but she knew how much money was coming in, where it was coming from, and when it would arrive from some of the assistance programs that we were enrolled in. She knew whether it was scheduled on a weekly, biweekly, or monthly basis. In between those times, she was an expert at making things stretch. If money wasn't available, she used her reputation to get what she needed.

When my mom, or "momma" as I referred to her, would send me to the neighborhood convenience store, most times she would give me a list of items to get but didn't give me money to get them with. I was only around 10 or 11 years old then. She would purchase them on what I call reputational credit, not with a credit card, but with telling the clerk I was sent by her name. Of course, they all knew who she was. Experiencing this for the first time went like this: She would call me into the room or kitchen, tell me to get a pen and paper, and write down the items she needed. She would say, "Go to the store and pick me up two of these, one of these, and be sure to get this brand. Don't bring back the other brand. I want this one. And tell them I'll pay them on Friday." She would grab the piece of paper I wrote on, look it over (she recognized shapes of certain letters), fold it, and put it in my pocket.

My understanding based on past convenience store runs was that I needed something to buy those things with, money or food stamps. But I didn't question it. When I would arrive at the store and find the things she wanted on the shelves from the list, I'd place them on the counter and watch them ring up the items. "That'll be fourteen dollars and thirty-five cents, little man." I'd stand there looking at them, not knowing what to say, so I'd hand them the list and tell them, "My momma said she will give you the money on Friday." The clerk would look at me perplexed and go on to tell me that they couldn't do that, that they needed the money for those purchases now. I would insist still that was what my momma told me to tell them. Eventually, they would ask, "Who is your mother?" Once I told them whose kid I was, they would immediately begin bagging the grocery items, hand them to me, and tell me to tell my mom that it was fine, they'll see her on Friday. I made purchases simply based on my mom's name and reputation. And because I was her son, it was as if she was there buying the items herself because of our relationship. And I didn't have to pay a dime! So, I enjoyed the benefits of whatever items were purchased, too.

The kingdom of God works the same way. As believers, we have been given authorization by Jesus the King. We have been given authority to sanction anything this earth has because God has given us dominion and rule over it. Yet, we are under the authority of Jesus as our King or the Godhead, and we are His body. As His body, we are to carry out the king's mandates and requests on earth as an extension of His will. And just like when I was on a mission to retrieve items with no money based on what my mother said, we are to receive our instructions from the headquarters of Heaven and carry out the mission of Heaven's agenda on earth, which is to tell the good news to the poor. In doing so, we get to enjoy the benefits of fulfilling the assignment given and the tools or resources necessary to effectively accomplish the desired call asked of us.

When we show love to one and other, we are demonstrating God's love. When we show character and integrity, we are putting Heaven on display. When we show and demonstrate that our needs and wants are met by sharing from our overflow, we are emulating the abundant nature of God as He provides for his children. In turn, we depict God's giving and rewarding nature, demonstrating that He is not a deadbeat dad!

WHY DOES THIS MATTER?

God's reputation and promises are on the line when we are not living according to what His word says. Likewise, when a king puts out a new mandate or law, it is to be carried out, no questions asked. He doesn't do what he says himself. Instead, it's to be carried out by his loyal and faithful subjects. They are then given every tool and resource necessary because the king commands it. Again, the king's reputation is on the line. Look at it from a manufacturer's product-recall perspective.

A product recall is a process of retrieving defective and/or potentially unsafe goods from consumers while providing those consumers with a fix of the defect or equal compensation. Recalls often occur because of safety concerns over a manufacturing defect in a product that may harm its user. In the automobile industry, for example, this happens with all makes and models of vehicles from time to time, because the safety of cars is important to both consumers and the manufacturer. These recalls help prevent future liabilities. When vehicle equipment poses a safety risk to drivers, passengers, or other motorists, then it can be recalled, which is a very expensive process for the manufacturer.

First, the car manufacturer sends out notices to everyone who owns a specific make and model within a certain model year or years. Then, it specifies details within the notice of the issue that needs correcting or replacing. It should continue by saying that all the necessary work will be done at the manufacturer's expense and is of no cost to the vehicle owner. It is simply a matter of scheduling an appointment at the nearest local car dealership to get the work completed. With the millions of vehicles on the road that have been bought and sold within a certain period of years, why would a car manufacturer go through the trouble and enormous expense of trying to prevent a potential safety hazard and instating a recall program? It's because the manufacturer's name and reputation are on the line, and their brand and name matter. They realize that it is far more profitable and simply good business practice to head off a potential safety issue and less expensive to do so than run the risk of creating a huge civil lawsuit against them, sabotaging future product and vehicle sales, and ruining their public image.

God is no different. When His children are not living the abundant life that Jesus promised in John 10:10 (AMP), "The thief comes only in order to steal and kill and destroy. I came that they may have and enjoy life, and have it in abundance [to the full, till it overflows]."

Or maybe His children are not experiencing what's said in Proverbs 10:22 (AMPC): "The blessing of the Lord—it makes [truly] rich, and He adds no sorrow with it [neither does toiling increase it]." Or John 14:14 (NIV): "You may ask me for anything in my name, and I will do it."

Or John 16:23 (NIV): "Very truly I tell you, my Father will give you whatever you ask in my name." Or Ephesians 3:20 (AMPC): "Now to Him Who, by [in consequence of] the [action of His] power that is at work within us, is able to [carry out His purpose and] do superabundantly, far over and above all that we [dare] ask or think [infinitely beyond our highest prayers, desires, thoughts, hopes, or dreams]." And if it does not happen, then we make God a liar and, in turn, we ruin His reputation.

BY GOD'S AUTHORITY

We look to Jesus as the example and the ambassador of everything the higher self brings to earth because He is the Author and Finisher of our faith in God's word. Study and act upon what He proclaimed as good news to everyone and emulate His teachings of righteousness so that you can effectively transform your soul to match the power within you and be all that you were created to be on earth. In other words, He came here to show you and me what the Kingdom of God looks like on earth and how it works. When He spoke, He spoke confidently in what He was saying. He spoke in love, and He spoke as if He was on an assignment—because He was. And His assignment was to demonstrate the power of your true higher form of self as you were created to function and perform. So, by faith, we, like Him, are also on assignment. And it is our job to release God's will into this earth—not in our name, but in the name, power, and glory of the Kingdom of God by Jesus, the Lord. We have been given legal right and authority to do whatever we ask of Him according to Heaven's will, and it will be done on earth as it is in Heaven. Jesus said it this way in Matthew 16:19 (NIV): "I will give you the keys of the Kingdom of Heaven; whatever you [legally] bind on earth will be bound in heaven, and whatever you lose on earth will be loosed in heaven." Just like I did when momma sent me to the convenience store with no money but in her name.

You are the vessel and the ambassador on earth who exercises that supreme authority of the Kingdom of God through the power and guidance of the Holy Spirit. This is how you prosper in everything and in every way. God cannot and will not perform anything on earth without doing it through you. You are a part of His body. Therefore, you have the authority to carry out His will and all of Heaven will back you up!

But to have authority, you must first respect and understand authority, which means you are to submit and be under authority and orders when the circumstance requires you to do so. If you cannot obey and respect the earthly authority God has put in place and the role in which you are put under—whether it's government authority, police authority, your boss or manager's authority, your pastor or spiritual leader's authority, your parents' authority, or even your husband or wife's authority—then God cannot trust you with the true authority you have been given by Him, which is His spirit. That makes you a rebel spirit! What happens to rebels? They will be kept in check financially or positionally until they decide of their own will and choosing to submit and follow instructions with obedience. Once the rebel is put under controlled guidance and is willing to follow with a submissive heart, then His spirit will flow into their hearts and minds to soften it and check for sincerity to follow His guidance. Then and only then can a changed rebel experience God's wisdom and power to produce the best of what He has for them in this life. We are ambassadors on this earth, sent by God under the authority of Christ Himself. We do and say what the Spirit of God says. If anyone asks you by whose authority, tell them you were sent by King Jesus. Don't attempt to perform or say anything that was not given to you first by God. This is the way of the profit. The following passages show what man does have authority over when operating by the awareness and power of the higher self.

THE POWER TO OVERCOME DEMONS, DARKNESS, AND EVIL

Luke 10:19 (AMPC) says, "Behold! I have given you authority and power to trample upon serpents and scorpions, and [physical and mental strength and ability] over all the power that the enemy [possesses]; and nothing shall in any way harm you."

Mark 16:17 (AMPC) says, "And these attesting signs will accompany those who believe in My name they will drive out demons."

James 4:7 (AMPC) says, "So be subject to God. Resist the devil [stand firm against him], and he will flee from you."

ANGELS TO ASSIST YOU WITH HEAVEN'S ARMED FORCES

Daniel 3:28 (AMPC) says, "Then Nebuchadnezzar said, 'Blessed be the God of Shadrach, Meshach, and Abednego, who has sent His angel and delivered

His servants who believed in, trusted in, and relied on Him!' And they set aside the king's command and yielded their bodies rather than serve or worship any god except their own God."

Matthew 26:53 (AMPC): "Do you suppose that I cannot appeal to My Father, and He will immediately provide Me with more than twelve legions [more than 80,000] of angels?"

Acts 12:7 (AMPC): "And suddenly an angel of the Lord appeared [standing beside him], and a light shone in the place where he was. And the angel gently smote Peter on the side and awakened him, saying, 'Get up quickly!' And the chains fell off his hands."

HEALING SICKNESSES AND DISEASES

Matthew 8:8–9 (AMPC): "But the centurion replied to Him, 'Lord, I am not worthy or fit to have You come under my roof; but only speak the word, and my servant boy will be cured. For I also am a man subject to authority, with soldiers subject to me. And I say to one, Go, and he goes; and to another, Come, and he comes; and to my slave, Do this, and he does it.'"

Matthew 8:13 (AMPC): "Then to the centurion Jesus said, 'Go; it shall be done for you as you have believed.' And the servant boy was restored to health at that very moment."

Mark 3:10 (AMPC): "For He had healed so many that all who had distressing bodily diseases kept falling upon Him and pressing upon Him in order that they might touch Him."

Acts 4:13–14 (AMPC): "Now when they saw the boldness and unfettered eloquence of Peter and John and perceived that they were unlearned and untrained in the schools [common men with no educational advantages], they marveled; and they recognized that they had been with Jesus. And since they saw the man who had been cured standing there beside them, they could not contradict the fact or say anything in opposition."

THE ANIMAL KINGDOM

Genesis 1:26 (AMPC): "God said, 'Let Us [Father, Son, and Holy Spirit] make mankind in Our image, after Our likeness, and let them have complete authority over the fish of the sea, the birds of the air, the [tame] beasts, and over all of the earth, and over everything that creeps upon the earth.'"

Acts 28:3 (AMPC), "Now Paul had gathered a bundle of sticks, and he was laying them on the fire when a viper crawled out because of the heat and fastened itself on his hand."

Verse 5: "Then [Paul simply] shook off the small creature into the fire and suffered no evil effects."

THE ELEMENTS: EARTH, WIND, FIRE, AND WATER

2 Kings 1:10 (AMPC): "Elijah said to the captain of fifty, 'If I am a man of God, then let fire come down from heaven and consume you and your fifty.' And fire fell from heaven and consumed him and his fifty."

Matthew 8:26 (AMPC): "And He said to them, 'Why are you timid and afraid, O you of little faith?' Then He got up and rebuked the winds and the sea, and there was a great and wonderful calm [a perfect peaceableness]."

DEATH BEFORE ITS TIME

John 11:41–44 (AMPC): "So they took away the stone. And Jesus lifted up His eyes and said, 'Father, I thank You that You have heard Me. Yes, I know You always hear and listen to Me, but I have said this on account of and for the benefit of the people standing around, so that they may believe that You did send Me [that You have made Me Your messenger].' When He had said this, He shouted with a loud voice, 'Lazarus, come out!' And out walked the man who had been dead, his hands and feet wrapped in burial cloths [linen strips], and with a [burial] napkin bound around his face. Jesus said to them, 'Free him of the burial wrappings and let him go.'"

Luke 8:52 and 55 (AMPC): "And all were weeping for and bewailing her; but He said, 'Do not weep, for she is not dead but sleeping.' And grasping her hand, He called, saying, 'Child, arise [from the sleep of death]!' And her spirit returned [from death], and she arose immediately."

1 Corinthians 15:26 (AMPC): "The last enemy to be subdued and abolished is death."

If Jesus did it, then you and I can do it, too. In fact, He said it Himself in John 14:12 (NIV): "Very truly I tell you, whoever believes in me will do the works I have been doing, and they will do even greater things than these..." I'm sure if this was not a true statement then He wouldn't have said it. And He wasn't just referring to the people He was talking to; He was referring to *whomever believes in Him*. If you're on the planet, then you are included and so am I. All it takes is stepping out of your comfort zone in who you think you are and beginning to operate in who and what you **know** you are, and you'll be able to witness and perform what many would call the impossible, too.

WHAT IS THE BELIEVER'S AUTHORITY?

When Jesus gave power and authority over spiritual darkness to the disciples, He also gave this power to all believers. This authority is available through faith. Spiritual authority is the mantle or rights from Heaven to use the name of Jesus through faith to do the task you've been given, just like a police officer. Under the Tenth Amendment to the United States Constitution, the powers not delegated to the federal government are reserved to the states or to the people.[51] Therefore, police power is defined in each jurisdiction by the legislative body, which determines the public purposes that need to be served by legislation. Once an officer has been sworn in, they become the authority within that jurisdiction to exercise and enforce the laws given by the state.

Imagine an officer witnessing a crime. Because they have been given authority already to act as an extension of the law enforced, they do not have to ask for permission to engage on behalf of the city or the state; they have already been authorized to do so. If a situation involves clearing traffic so that a life-flight helicopter can land in the middle of a busy street, they have the authority to make everyone comply and bend to their will, because the will is the same as the will of the laws of that jurisdiction. Even if a semitruck is coming in at full speed, they have the authority to stop that driver and truck by standing in the middle of the road with their hand out, signaling them to stop the vehicle in the name of the law. Their uniform and badge show that they are authorized to do so. The believer's authority is no different. You are authorized to act in

---

51   "Tenth Amendment," Cornell Law School Legal Information Institute, accessed August 9, 2021, https://www.law.cornell.edu/constitution/tenth_amendment.

any situation that involves bending the will to the power given, including replenishing resources that are lacking for someone in need.

This was demonstrated in the 6th chapter of Mark when Jesus fed more than 5,000 people who were on hand and had followed him and his disciples into the desert to hear Him speak. They were out there so long that the disciples requested that the people be sent home before they didn't have enough energy to get back to where they came from. Jesus suggested that the disciples feed them, and their response was logically one of surprise and confusion to such an overwhelming request. They said to Him in verse 37 (NIV), "That would take more than half a year's wages! Are we to go and spend that much on bread and give it to them to eat?" They equated feeding 5,000-plus people to the level of expense needed to do such a thing, but Jesus responded to the economic dilemma by multiplying resources with what they had currently available.

This is a lesson to both you and me that problems or concerns that involve money or supply can certainly be addressed and solved through divine means. Jesus knew what to do because he understood both the natural laws of the earth and the spiritual laws of the divine. As a believer, you must understand the divine laws just like a police officer understands legislative laws. Knowing your rights within the authority you've been granted can save the lives of both you and whomever is involved. The opposite is also true—not knowing your authority or the laws you've been granted can be a hindrance or a detriment in a given situation and can become a liability or a fatality depending on the circumstances.

Whether it's your authority to execute natural laws or divine laws, neither law is obligated to comply or bend to your will because of your lack of understanding or your incorrectly applying them. By not understanding both or either, the results are the opposite of the intent you imposed. Imagine not knowing that electricity and water don't mix. That's potentially a fatal lesson that you may not get to course-correct if applied wrong. On the other hand, think of salt. Pure salt consists of the elements sodium and chloride. Sodium is essential to human health, but too much sodium is poisonous.[52] Sodium

---

52   "Sodium in Your Diet," U.S. Food & Drug Administration (FDA), June 8, 2021, https://www. fda.gov/food/nutrition-education-resources-materials/sodium-your-diet.

poisoning can cause seizures, coma, and death.[53] However, when sodium is mixed with chloride, you get a tasty combination of minerals that can spice up a bland meal. This simple combination mixed incorrectly doesn't mean that the minerals themselves are supposed to give you a break for not knowing how to use them. Depending on the circumstance, not knowing can not only hurt you, but in some cases, it can kill you.

These same principles apply to wealth building. Yes, some practicalities can get you far financially, and many use these principles in everyday operation. A percentage of those who are disciplined may reap a reward over time with the right applications and combinations of managing, saving, and investing. However, those disciplines alone are no match for the root causes of the spiritual dark forces that can eat away at your efforts over a lifetime or even generations. If they are not addressed and you are oblivious to the root cause of why things seem to go south as soon as you gain a little momentum in wealth building, then like the ignorance of natural laws, you'll never get ahead and will blame it on bad luck, bad breaks, where you're from, your upbringing, your family, or somebody else.

You have the authority, and wealth is laid up for you and in you. It is in your nature to be wealthy, and you have the right and the go-ahead from your Creator to do so from within your higher self.

---

53   Libby Mitchell, "Risks of Salt Poisoning," University of Utah Healthcare, August 5, 2016, https://healthcare.utah.edu/healthfeed/postings/2016/08/salt_poisoning.php.

SECTION III: THE WAY IS LAW

CHAPTER 9

UNIVERSAL LAWS

"When money realizes that it is in good hands, it wants to stay and multiply in those hands."

—Idowu Koyenikan[54]

When my mom and dad were together, family time was fun. As I've mentioned before, both my mom and dad had a good sense of humor, and sadly, they both thought they were funny. They had different styles, for sure, but they were hilarious nonetheless. Of course, this behavior rubbed off on my siblings and me.

Some of the most memorable moments were during holidays, birthdays, and most Sundays. For example, during Christmas and Thanksgiving, my mom always made her signature homemade peanut brittle candy. It was the best brittle candy I've ever tasted. Even today, I'd be hard-pressed to find anything even close to how good hers was, from what I remember. Overall, she was an excellent cook, and she was so proud when everyone would beg her to make

---

54   Tweet   by   @IlkElevates,   October   6,   2018,   https://twitter.com/IkElevates/status/1048740704246272000.

certain meals. Unfortunately, the candy was only made and set aside specifically for the holidays. One of the family rituals that signified she was in the process of making the candy was when she would come home with a huge sack of fresh shelled peanuts. We all had to pitch in to crack open the peanut shells one by one, deshell the nuts, and put them on a large tray.

Fresh peanuts have a reddish skin on them that can be tedious to remove by hand to get to the clean waxy peanuts you see in a jar at the grocery store. To remedy this, my mom would put the peanuts on a large tray and bake them until the outer skin layers became dry and brittle. Then later at night, we would take the tray with the mountain of peanuts on it, go outside while it was windy, and walk around the house to allow the wind to blow through the tray and separate the dried skin coverings from the nuts while we shook the tray like a sifting tool. It was ingenious! The key was to walk exactly three times around the house and no running. This little procedure made the candy even more satisfying to us kids, because we felt we all had a small role in making her signature brittle with her.

Another activity we did together as a family was movie night once a month at the drive-in theater. The snacks and treats were the same: Bugle corn chips, popcorn, candy bars, sodas, and sandwiches. All seven of us would pile into the car after my dad got home from work. Sometimes we invited the neighbors' kids to come along with us.

My wife's family, on the other hand, didn't practice many family traditions that she can recall. They did celebrate holidays like Christmas when they exchanged gifts, but no activities that were regularly practiced beyond that that could be considered a family tradition. Upon learning this when we were dating, I wanted to ensure her that when we married and decided to have a family of our own, we would incorporate traditions together as a couple that would express joy and build memories for ourselves and our children. And that is exactly what we did.

For the holidays, we all dress up to express our appreciation for how blessed we are. Giving thanks individually during Thanksgiving is especially important to us. During gatherings with our extended family, it's a known family tradition that there will be a *Soul Train* dance line that you must participate in before you leave the gathering to go home. The rule applies whether you can dance or not. It's such a tradition that when my daughter was planning her wedding with her now-husband, he was a nervous wreck the week before the wedding because he and his family, including his mom and dad, knew they were going to have to participate and dance in the *Soul Train* line. (If you don't know what a *Soul Train* line is, do a YouTube search for Don Cornelius and the *Soul Train*.) Our kids love this tradition, and I'm sure it will be passed on to their children.

Family traditions, for some, are very important. They bring a sense of to-getherness and identity to the members involved that say you are a part of something special or exclusive. While traditions are kept and carried out for generations in some families, they are, of course, not mandatory to adhere to, yet traditions are considered to be a type of rule, constant, or law.

FOUR TYPES OF LAWS

Like traditions, some other laws have been created to allow humans to gather either in unison with a belief or to keep a level of order and decorum in society. Four types of laws are: traditional or ritual law, legislative law, natural law, and supernatural or spiritual law,[55] with each law having more weight or power than the preceding laws. For example, if a conflict exists between individuals or a group of people concerning the rules of compliance with their traditional law, then legislative law will settle the dispute. This way, the rule of the legislative law supersedes the traditional law and bends the will of the people by bringing everyone into compliance with the rules and consequences the legislative law carries. All parties involved benefit in some way or capacity, allowing each person to live, express, and create the kind of life they want within those legal boundaries. Step out of those boundaries, and the law will work against you.

TRADITIONAL LAW

Traditional law, also known as customary law, is defined as a belief or be-havior (folk custom) passed down within a group or society with symbolic meaning or special significance with origins in the past. As defined by the

---

55 Munroe Global, "Understanding The 4 Types of Laws | Dr Myles Munroe," YouTube video, October 18, 2020, https://www.youtube.com/watch?v=VlPp6KVs0ZQ.

World Intellectual Property Organization (WIPO), customary law is a "set of customs, practices and beliefs that are accepted as obligatory rules of conduct" by indigenous peoples and local communities.[56] Customary law forms an intrinsic part of social and economic systems and way of life. Common examples include holidays, our family Soul Train lines, or socially meaningful but impractical clothes (like lawyers' wigs or military officers' spurs), but the idea has also been applied to social norms such as greetings.

Traditions can persist and evolve for thousands of years. The word "tradition" itself is derived from the Latin word "*tradere*," which means to transmit, to hand over, or to give for safekeeping.[57] While it is commonly assumed that traditions have an ancient history, many traditions have been invented on purpose, whether that be political or cultural, over short periods. Nevertheless, traditions exist and are practiced every year somewhere all over the world.

LEGISLATIVE LAW

Legislation refers to the "preparation and enactment of laws by a legislative body through its lawmaking process." The legislative process includes evaluating, amending, and voting on proposed laws and is concerned with the words used in the bill to communicate the values, judgments, and purposes of the proposal. A bill is a draft, or tentative version, of what might become part of the written law. A bill that is enacted is called an act or statute.[58] In the U.S., "once the bill is approved by both houses and is put into final form, it must be signed by the executive. An executive can refuse to sign a bill and can return it to the legislature with a veto message explaining why. If the executive signs the bill, it is filed and becomes law."[59] Once it's law, all citizens must comply.

---

56   "Customary Law and Intellectual Property," World Intellectual Property Organization (WIPO), accessed August 10, 2021, https://www.wipo.int/tk/en/indigenous/customary_law/index.html.

57   "tradition (n.)," Online Etymology Dictionary, accessed August 10, 2021, https://www.etymonline.com/word/tradition.

58   "Legislation," Cornell Law School Legal Information Institute, accessed August 10, 2021, https://www.law.cornell.edu/wex/legislation.

59   Ibid.

Legislative law has all governing power within a society. However, in a democratic society, laws are usually enacted based on majority rule. This is problematic, because if the majority of people feels it is important to pass a certain type of law, then it becomes law simply because the minority is outnumbered by the majority. Then what happens if the majority is corrupt? Good people will suffer under a corrupt majority-ruled system of legislative law. What if the majority decides to pass a law like in the Hollywood movie *The Purge*, where there's a legally specified day where everyone gets to break any law without penalty or consequences for that day?[60] That would be a horrible law. But if the majority agreed to pass such a law, then your life can be in danger. However, legislative law does not, nor cannot, combat or redirect natural law.

NATURAL LAW

Natural laws, also referred to as laws of nature, are permanent. Theory in ethics and philosophy says that human beings possess a fundamental value system that governs our reasoning and behavior. These rules of right and wrong are inherent in all of us. Legislation or government intervention is not involved. Instead, these rules supersede legislative law. It's this part of us that, by divine instinct, tells us that there is something bigger and greater than ourselves. This void or curiosity within us is what causes us to search deeper within ourselves to find meaning and purpose. This deep search is what draws us into identifying our original true spiritual selves, thus reconnecting back to God. However, awareness alone cannot help us tap into the greatest part of ourselves; we must pursue it with intention. And that is how we discover there is more to us than our experiences—an inherited super nature within us.

Natural law also deals with the laws of nature and our surroundings on earth and in the universe. By nature, the laws of physics suggest to us that the world around us works a certain way, and physical laws are a way of classifying those workings. Physical laws are just conclusions drawn based on years of scientific observations and experiments, which are repeated over and over under different conditions to reach conclusions that can be accepted around the world. These are continuously validated by the scientific community over time. Once these findings are validated, they can then be deemed as constants

---

60   *The Purge*, dir. James DeMonaco, Blumhouse Productions, 85 mins. (2013).

of our atmosphere—meaning that we can depend on certain things like seasons, gravity, air supply, sunrises, sunsets, the rotation of the earth on its axis, and so on. For example, we're never going to wake up one morning and see everything floating in the air because there was a gravity issue. Gravity is dependable. These same dependable principles can also be applied to creating formulas for both success and failure.

SUPERNATURAL LAW

The physical laws that govern our universe are constant, unchanging, and essential for life. The unseen spiritual laws are the same but are far more powerful and important. Supernatural laws are also permanent, and they supersede all laws because all laws are derived from the spirit realm. All things were thoughts first, or all things are manifested thoughts. All visible things were invisible first, and divine laws are the invisible workings that create, manifest, and bound natural law together and in place. For reference, the Bible makes this claim clear in the following passages.

Hebrews 11:3 (AMPC) says, "By faith we understand that the worlds [during the successive ages] were framed [fashioned, put in order, and equipped for their intended purpose] by the word of God, so that what we see was not made out of things which are visible."

Romans 1:20 (AMPC) says, "For ever since the creation of the world His invisible nature and attributes, that is, His eternal power and divinity, have been made intelligible and clearly discernible in and through the things that have been made [His handiworks]. So [men] are without excuse [altogether without any defense or justification]."

John 1:3 (AMPC): "All things were made and came into existence through Him; and without Him was not even one thing made that has come into being."

And lastly, Colossians 1:16–17 (AMPC): "For it was in Him that all things were created, in heaven and on earth, things seen and things unseen, whether thrones, dominions, rulers, or authorities; all things were created and exist through Him [by His service, intervention] and in and for Him. And He

Himself existed before all things, and in Him all things consist [cohere, are held together]."

GET THE LAW ON YOUR SIDE

As a young man, I had my share of traffic violations while driving. And based on experience, I can tell you traffic tickets are not fun. Disputing them in court is even worse. Wait, let me back up and start over. Until a few years ago, I'd had my share of driving tickets, and I can tell you based on experience, traffic tickets are not fun and disputing them in court is even worse. It's a drain on your time and money, and it's a drain on your self-esteem. I've been to traffic hearings so many times that I kind of get the flow of how the system operates. For instance, I know that if the police officer who pulled you over and gave you the citation does not show up in court for the case to be called, your case is dismissed. For that reason alone, I never pled guilty, because I wasn't. Well, maybe I was, but I just didn't see it that way. Nevertheless, when I would appear in court, I would pray that the officer would not show up. It was about a fifty-fifty chance either way. Regardless, it was still a big waste of my time.

It wasn't until a few years ago that I discovered that as some people were going through to approach the judge and turn in their pleas, they had an attorney representing them. I also noticed that for those who had attorneys, a lot of them didn't have to show up for court in person and the cases were dropped, one after another. My only reason for opting against legal representation was that I assumed it was too expensive for the violation. Who needs an attorney when I could dispute it myself? Besides, driving school and other alternatives were sometimes offered so that I could trade for that instead of allowing the judgment to go on my state's driving record. Still, it was a lot of my time taken away from me, and as a busy father and husband who worked for a living, time was money. Once I researched the idea of having a traffic attorney, to my surprise, it wasn't that expensive at all. It was less expensive than the violation itself. Also, I didn't have to show up for court in person because my attorney was my represented replacement. It was such a thrill to hear that my case was dismissed or that the charges were dropped whether the officer appeared or not. Either way, I was exonerated. That's when I learned the value of hiring a lawyer to represent me. Having representation that understood the laws and how to communicate effectively to the judge made all the difference. It saved me money, time, energy, and valuable resources for a problem that had an easy solution.

This example is no different than understanding the principles of spiritual law. When trying to do something in your natural strength or limited understanding, personal relationships in natural circumstances will usually bring you a slow, painful, time-consuming result, because natural law is governed by time. Supernatural law is not governed by time. More than that, supernatural law supersedes natural laws! By understanding the laws of the supernatural or divine, positive outcomes can happen much sooner and quicker for you than working within the natural realm—sometimes on a much larger and more profound scale. Here's what I mean.

Most major cities that have highways and freeways may also have high-occupancy vehicle (HOV) lanes. These lanes are designated for driving commuters who have agreed to carpool with two or more passengers. They were created to help decrease traffic congestion during high traffic times, like early mornings and late afternoons.

A Texas A&M 2021 Urban Mobility Report ranked the city of Houston as having the third worst traffic flow of U.S. cities.[61] New York-Newark was ranked as the worst.[62] No matter which direction you live in Houston, you're bound to run into heavy traffic during peak traffic hours. However, if you have multiple passengers in the vehicle with you, you qualify for the HOV lanes. Depending on how far you'll have to drive each day, you can shave off 15 to 45 minutes of your commute time. By qualifying for the HOV lanes, you automatically receive the benefits of saving time. All it takes is understanding what's necessary to comply and put the knowledge in motion. Like the HOV lane example, spiritual law works the same way. You must first understand divine law, determine the benefits, apply the necessary actions or

---

61   David Schrank et al., "2021 Urban Mobility Report," The Texas A&M Transportation Institute with cooperation from INRIX, June 2021, https://static.tti.tamu.edu/tti.tamu.edu/documents/mobility-report-2021.pdf.

62   Ibid.

steps to put it in motion, and you'll get the manifestation of what it governs in the earth realm.

Here's an example of divine law in my own life using my oldest daughter's experience. When she was about the age of 10, she asked me to help her find a way to earn some extra money. I asked her how much extra money she was seeking and what she wanted it for. She went on to tell me she would like to have $10 but she didn't want her mom or me to give it to her. She wanted to somehow earn it. With that in mind, she asked about extra things she could do around the house or something that she could do for me that would earn her the amount she wanted. Instead, I decided to show her how to put divine law into motion for what she wanted. I explained it in very simple terms she could understand. I told her, "If you want $10, you have to know and imagine what you're going to do with it." She said she wasn't sure. I preceded to ask her what were all the things she thought she would *want* to do with the money. She began to think about all the possibilities, like buying candy or a toy or dining at a fine restaurant. Whatever it was, I told her to keep thinking about those things.

Once she settled on an item, it was time to take action. I asked her if she understood why we give to people. She replied, "Yes, to help them." I asked, "How does that make you feel when you help someone?" She said it felt good. I said, "You know why it feels good? Because it makes God want to do something good for you for being more like Him. This is why when you give something it comes back to you with more." I went on to suggest, "Let's take whatever you have and let's plant it into something to help people. If you have a dollar, let's take that dollar and put it into the offering plate when we go to church. Right now, they need help to build a school for special needs children. I think that would be a great thing to put money towards." She agreed.

At church, when the offering time was near before, we put what she had into the offering tray, but we spoke over it first: "This seed is planted to help the children in need. Also, it would be nice if in return for her generosity, she receives $10 back to her to have fun with, to buy things with it, or use it to give to someone else." We then put the $1 into the offering bucket, and we went away believing wholeheartedly that somehow, she would get $10 or even more in return. She was so excited. By the way, if you're with the "You don't give to get" crowd, I'll address that in a later chapter.

Because I wanted her to see for herself how this principle works, I resisted everything I could to not give the $10 to her myself. See, it's paternal nature. Later that evening, a neighbor from the other side of the block called us on the phone. It was my daughter's friend's mom. She asked if she could ask my daughter for a favor and went on to say that she needed someone to feed a new pet they had while they were gone away for a few days on vacation, since they could not bring their pets with them. She said she would gladly pay for the much needed help. I asked my daughter if that would be something she could do for them, and she, of course, replied with a big YES! After ending the call, I quickly reminded her about the money she gave to help the children and how her generosity was coming back to her—but only because of what we spoke and agreed to over it.

When the pet project was completed, my daughter received $25 for the job, which was more than she wanted. Furthermore, these neighbors didn't own a pet until a day before they called us. They explained to us how a stray cat came wandering from out of nowhere into their yard and just laid there on the front lawn. Since it had no tags or collars and no one claimed it, they took it in as their own. Without thinking ahead, they completely forgot they were going on vacation the next few days. So, because they had not planned on having a pet, they called my daughter for help.

This stray cat could have laid in anyone's yard. Instead, it walked over to a home that took it in as their own, and that family just so happens to know my family. The timing of the cat arriving in combination with the timing of them going on vacation and my daughter's desire for extra money all came together, divinely setting the law of giving and receiving in motion.

This is just one small example of how the law of reciprocity works. There are many different spiritual and divine laws that are available to anyone and everyone at any time for anything. It's just a matter of knowing the laws exist and putting them to work for you. This same law my little daughter put in motion works regardless of the amount, whether it's for $10, $1,000, $100,000, $500,000, $1,000,000, or $500 million. It doesn't matter. By using the law and the power of belief and submitting to the process and guidance of the spirit, you can watch the laws of the divine work for you, too, for anything.

CHAPTER 10

DIVINE LAWS FOR WEALTH

You create your thoughts; your thoughts create your intentions and your intentions create your reality.

—*Wayne Dyer*[63]

I used one small example of how the law of giving and receiving, also known as the law of reciprocity, produces results. In this chapter, I want to highlight a few of the most important divine laws that pertain to building wealth. Provided is a description of what the law is and why it works—beginning with the law I used with my daughter, which was the law of reciprocity.

THE LAW OF RECIPROCITY

The law of reciprocity is also known as the law of giving and receiving. In social psychology, reciprocity is a process of exchanging things with other people in order to gain a mutual benefit.[64] I'm sure you've experienced this law at

---

63   Wayne Dyer, *Everyday Wisdom* (Carlsbad, CA: Hay House, 2005).

64   Kendra Cherry, "What is Reciprocity?" Verywellmind, updated may 26, 2020, https://www.verywellmind.com/what-is-the-rule-of-reciprocity-2795891.

work on occasion at some point in your life. Think about this for a moment. When someone has done something nice for you without your prompting or even suggesting they do so, have you ever noticed that you feel compelled to do something for them in return? There's something in you that seems to compel a deep-rooted psychological urge to return the kind gesture or action they displayed to you. As a matter of fact, you may even reciprocate with a gesture far more generous than their original good deed. I can't tell you how many times I've tipped a waiter or waitress far more then I intended to when I felt the level of service exceeded my expectations. This compulsion or *wanting* to do so is the spiritual law of reciprocity in action.

WHY IT MATTERS

You can try and resist this law, but as spiritual beings, you will more than likely still feel that you need to respond in kind to a good deed. This is because the law of reciprocity is built into your super nature. It's the God part of you that wants to respond in kind. Remember, one of the characteristics of God is to reward. It's the golden rule: Treat others the way you would want to be treated, which you can find in Mathew 7:12 (AMP): "So then, in everything treat others the same way you want them to treat you, for this is [the essence of] the law and the [writings of the] Prophets." It's a law that sits in line with the entire universe because its creative motion is circular—meaning that whatever you give out, it will come back to you. So, if you want to put the operation of the law of reciprocity to work, give something. But be careful what you give out, whether good or bad, it's guaranteed to come back to you.

THE LAW OF FORGIVENESS

Forgiving yourself or someone else is an exercise of releasing or setting free the soul or the mind to work in harmony with the spirit. However, unforgiveness is quite the opposite. Unforgiveness is like hair in a drain or an obstruction in the way of a flowing river—when the spirit of truth wants to flow freely through your higher self, it finds roadblocks or impurities along the way to your soul. Imagine how liberated your soul would be if you did not burden your consciousness and others' with perceived wrongs, guilt, judgments, shame, slights, humiliations, or depravity for what you thought was lawfully yours? With forgiveness, we tell others that we no longer hold ourselves or them guilty. We pardon, absolve, and overlook everything that is stopping us from loving ourselves and others more.

Why It Matters

When we forgive, we are more like God. We are at peace and free to go on with life. We feel empowered and compassionate. The grip of the offense no longer controls our thoughts or actions in a negative way, allowing us to continue moving forward. In the same way, forgiveness frees up your giving. In fact, forgiving is for giving. Allow me to repeat it for you so that you truly understand it. Forgiving is FOR-GIVING. If there is one law that can cancel out the other, it is the law of unforgiveness. If you are holding anger, bitterness, strife, or any of the negative or base nature emotions against someone while you are giving or being generous, it will clog avenues that flow back to you for receiving by quieting your ability to hear the instructions on how to manifest from God's spirit. It will un-give your giving.

Mark 11:24 (AMP) says this, "For this reason I [Jesus] am telling you, whatever things you ask for in prayer [in accordance with God's will], believe [with confident trust] that you have **received** them, and they will be **given** to you." Notice he said whatever things you ask for, meaning that it does not matter what it is. If you put the laws to work, it will produce whatever you ask for according to God's will. But look at verse 25 where he goes on to say, "Whenever you stand praying, if you have anything against anyone, forgive him [drop the issue, let it go], so that your Father who is in Heaven will also forgive you your transgressions and wrongdoings [against Him and others]." The ruler and creator of all is the only judge of all things and is the author and creator of all divine laws. To put this in simple terms that anyone can understand, if unforgiving causes ungiving, then forgiving is also for-giving.

THE LAW OF WORDS

"Words are singularly the most powerful force available to humanity. We can choose to use this force constructively with words of encouragement, or destructively using words of despair. Words have energy and power with the ability to help, to heal, to hinder, to hurt, to harm, to humiliate and to humble." —Yehuda Berg[65]

Words are the spiritual containers that come from the depts of the soul and the spirit that carries out the mission of seeking, finding and returning the things or intentions to and for the author of them. Once again, words are set in perpetual and circular motion. Therefore, they are programmed to accomplish what has been uttered from the spirit vortex. Our spirit speaks in pictures and groans that are formulated and released through vibrations and sound. When we customize these vibrations with tone, pitch, and expression, we utter these formulated words into structural language. This communication medium allows another listening spirit, human or creation, to understand and carry out the words' intended mission.

Why It Matters

Dr. Hyder Zahed, a scientist, author, speaker, and regular contributor to *The Huffington Post*, said this about words: "Considering the 'powerful force' of the words we utter, we must discipline ourselves to speak in a way that conveys respect, gentleness and humility. One of the clearest signs of a moral life is right speech. Perfecting our speech is one of the keystones of mature people. Before speaking, take a few moments to contemplate what you will say and how you will say it; while considering the impact they will have on the listener(s)."[66]

Words are very powerful—so powerful that God used them to create all of existence. And if God used them to create, you and I can do the same.

THE LAW OF HONOR

Honor means to "weigh heavily," to highly esteem and respect the opinion or office of another. Usually, we learn what honor is by experiencing dishonor. We all know what it feels like to be disrespected, whether in words or in deeds, specifically when this person is supposed to be subjected to you, like your child, or if you're in a position of leadership, a subordinate. If you

---

65   Yehuda Berg, "The Power of Words," Huff Post, updated November 17, 2011, https://www.huffpost.com/entry/the-power-of-words_1_b_716183.

66   Hyder Zahed, "The Power of Spoken Words," Huff Post, December 15, 2014, https://www.huffpost.com/entry/the-power-of-spoken-words_b_6324786.

cannot respect or honor those who are placed above you—parents, supervisors, government officials, etc.—there is no way you can honor God without obeying Him. We must always give honor to whom honor is due, as Romans 13:7 (CEB) says, "So pay everyone what you owe them. Pay the taxes you owe, pay the duties you are charged, give respect to those you should respect, and honor those you should honor."

WHY IT MATTERS

When you are viewed as honorable, people trust the information you are providing, the company or organization you are representing, and the actions you are taking. Honor helps define who you are as a person. It also gives another person a peek into who you really are, your higher self. Showing honor gives light and serves as a guide for your spiritual growth and character.

THE LAW OF ABUNDANCE

This law is also known as the law of supply. Abundance is your natural state. It's provisions available to anyone that were created, long before the first man ever appeared on the earth. And like earth, Heaven is even more abundant with resources. Heaven has the supply that houses whatever you can possibly ever need and is stored up for you in abundance. If you truly believe that wealth and abundance is your natural state, your experiences in life will naturally lead you to this. You must shift your beliefs towards Heaven's abundance and not towards what your natural eyes perceive or the circumstances may imply. You must expect to receive any and everything you need with ease and flow.

WHY IT MATTERS

Heaven's economy is not based on legislation or swings of supply and demand. Whatever you can imagine within your spirit to need or want, you can access it to receive. Jesus said in Matthew 16:19 (NIV), "I will give you the keys of the kingdom of heaven. Whatever you bind on earth will be bound in heaven, and whatever you loose on earth will be loosed in heaven."

THE LAW OF ATTRACTION

What you focus your thoughts on expands. When you think of positive things, you accelerate the process of having positive experiences, particularly when you express gratitude for all the blessings you've already received. You attract into your life the people and circumstances that are in alignment with what you illuminate out into the world. Once you understand this law and begin to notice what you're paying attention to, you'll be able to create and shape the experiences you want in all areas of your life—including wealth.

Why It Matters

Ever heard the expression, "Trouble seems to always find me"? That expression is an example of how we are designed to attract. The same is true if you were to radiate joy, happiness, or wealth. It will seek out and attract what you emit. The law of attraction operates on thoughts, words, emotions, and actions, and it reflects back to you through experiences, like a signal or an airwave. The result is that you attract into your life the people and circumstances that are in alignment with what you radiate out into the world.

THE LAW OF GRATITUDE

This law is also known as the law of thanksgiving. Learning and practicing the law of gratitude will enhance the practice of the law of attraction. Gratitude is as an attitude of being thankful, being ready to show appreciation for anything received. It also includes returning the kindness. If you express gratitude, you will attract more reasons for expressing gratitude. Since your mind attracts more of what you focus your mind on, the more gratitude you express, the more you will be able to express. Likewise, the more misery you think about, the more you will attract into your life.

Why It Matters

As you continue to grow in your practice of gratitude, there will be more and more reasons to show your gratitude. Give God the honor He deserves by expressing gratitude and praise and watch how the law of reciprocity becomes activated almost immediately.

THE LAW OF VISUALIZATION

As humans, we think in pictures, not words. What we can *see* or picture in our minds, we tend to believe or act on. Visualization is a huge part of what you begin to believe. If you can't visualize it, it's quite hard to act on it. The visualization works both ways, positively and negatively, depending on what you perceive. Philippians 4:8 (CEB) says, "From now on, brothers and sisters, if anything is excellent and if anything is admirable, focus your thoughts on these things: all that is true, all that is holy, all that is just, all that is pure, all that is lovely, and all that is worthy of praise."

Why It Matters

When you take time to visualize, you're making time on purpose. Calming yourself from the inside out helps you learn how to control your thoughts. This is an important ability to have if you are constantly living in stressful situations. Visualization allows you to take control of what you are thinking about and how your body is reacting to those thoughts. Once your thoughts are under control, you can better govern your attitude and what you choose to believe.

THE LAW OF BELIEVING

I touched on faith in an earlier chapter and described it as Heaven's currency. Faith's value comes from love, and it is fueled and powered by belief. All things come from God and are made by God, and it is by faith that we participate through the divine to receive by the power of belief.

Remember, faith is a spirit (a noun) and is always present. We all have faith. Believing is the force from our spirit that thrusts our faith into the kingdom realm by what we see within ourselves, a force or power that literally moves things to cooperate with what we have believed. Or it moves us to move things.

Faith without belief is like a vehicle without an operator. They go hand in hand. Jesus said in Mark 11:22–24 (NIV), "Have faith in God. Truly I tell you, if anyone says to this mountain, 'Go, throw yourself into the sea,' and does not doubt in their heart but **believes** that what they **say** will happen, **it will be done for them**. Therefore, I tell you, whatever you ask for in prayer, **believe** that you have received it, and it will be yours." Your level of believing will determine your level of receiving.

Why It Matters

Faith's purpose is to do the impossible and immeasurable will of God on earth, based on what the spirit of God has commissioned you to say and do.

Spoken words are the containers or vehicles and believing is the fuel that propels your faith. Your role is to simply believe!

Learn to see through your eyes of belief, not just with your physical eyes but seeing spiritually deep inside of you. To renew your thoughts, you have to renew the way you visualize. Learn to see and trust possibilities rather than default to your past experiences of what seems impossible. Your brain is simply a processor of information, memories, learning, and experiences that helps you choose what to believe or not to believe. God's reality is always spirit first, not carnal or physical. Therefore, what you see as possible inside of you helps you produce renewed words in your speech.

You can't believe something wholeheartedly unless you can see it. Again, not physical sight but spiritual sight. You can't truly say what you don't believe. If God said it, then you should say it because it's possible. If God didn't say it, then you shouldn't say it because it may very well be impossible.

CHAPTER 11

WEALTH BY THE NUMBERS

"If people do not believe that mathematics is simple, it is only because they do not realize how complicated life is."

—*John von Neumann*[67]

Looking for a job is not fun! Whether it's for a short or long period of time, it doesn't matter—it's just not a great feeling knowing you have to search for another means of supply. I've certainly had my fair share of unemployment and when you're the primary breadwinner for the family, I can tell you firsthand, it's humiliating. The best part of those times for me was having a supportive and encouraging spouse. Even though she was primarily at home, homeschooling and taking care of all of us, she would still look for other ways she could help with the finances to help keep things afloat until I found something that could sustain us. In those times, it really helped. But still, it was my job to find something that would help get us back to the standard of living everyone was used to.

---

67   Franz L. Alt, "Archaeology of computers: Reminiscences, 1945--1947," *Communications of the ACM* 15, no. 7 (July 1972).

I remember one career search lasting far longer than I wanted it to. Usually, it didn't take me too long to find something else when we needed it. But this time was very different, probably because I was really praying for something more rewarding and specific. Long dry spells can really test your faith and resolve. It takes every bit of courage, faith, and sustained optimism to continue pushing past the rejection and false starts to continue through the search. It was during this time I discovered and joined a nonprofit group called In Between Job Ministries.

This organization was made up of a group of volunteers who went through their own journeys of career hunting. With the help of others who encouraged them through those times, they dedicated their own time and energy to helping others as an act of giving back or paying it forward, ministering to people and reminding them they were worthy of finding the right career path with confidence and educating them along the way.

They also allowed hiring employers on the campus who were looking for qualified candidates with the right skill set for *on-the-spot* interviews. I was impressed with the tireless quality of care and professionalism they displayed to anyone who needed help. Even today, I am grateful for the experience and the expression of love poured into me personally, strengthening my inner man and helping me to believe that the right thing was going to open up for me. It's one of the sole reasons why I give back my time and resources for as many people as I can during those tough times. If you aren't familiar with this ministry, I highly recommend you research them and support their cause.

My job search during that time was a little tricky because what I desired was not easily found when doing a random search on the internet. You see, I was a sales and business consultant prior to my unemployment, and those roles were few to none. To complicate matters, I was in a specific industry, the automobile business, that didn't translate too well into other industries. While I had a stellar reputation personally, the industry itself did not. Over time, effort with few to no responses to my inquiries began to take a toll on my confidence. After a few months, I began sinking into a really low mental and emotional place of consciousness. But I soldiered on.

Even though my wife found something temporarily to help fill the gap in the meantime, I could tell she didn't enjoy it, which was completely understandable. After all, home was her career that she loved and working outside of the home was my job.

Right before I found what I considered to be the perfect job at the time, I remember distinctly mustering up the courage in prayer to talk to the Lord about what was truly my heart's desire.

I could sense in my spirit God asking me what it was that I really wanted and to write it down on paper. I knew the first five or six items immediately. I wrote them down quickly in the following order.

MY CAREER: THE 10 THINGS I WANT MOST

1. Income (I wrote down a very specific amount here).

2. Working no nights or weekends.

3. A company vehicle.

4. I want to work from home (and not have a daily commute).

5. Full health and medical benefits for me and the family.

6. Travel to different cities, states, or countries.

7. Stay within my same industry as a consultant. No selling.

8. A company expense account (in the past as a consultant, I had to pay for my own expenses).

9. An office assistant for tracking expenses and booking travel.

10. Earn travel points and miles for vacations.

That was my list. At the time, I figured if I'm going to be honest with myself and with God in prayer, I might as well lay it all out there, holding nothing back. I believed what I wrote down existed because I've known people who were doing it. I just wasn't confident it would happen for me. But I was going to forge ahead anyway.

One morning on my way to Between Jobs Ministry, my sister wanted to come with me. I told her about the ministry and how the people were so generous and helpful that she should come since she was looking for something in education. During one of the many group and course meetings they provided, I attended the Elevator Pitch meeting. This group helped attendees learn valuable interview and resume-writing skills. Once those items were completed, they demonstrated how to do elevator pitches. Since I also had a background as a career's recruiter, I thought it would be interesting to listen to some of the members of the group give their testimonies and pitch. There were times employers would attend, but I didn't have much faith in the fact that someone would talk about anything close to what I was looking for.

Looking at the time on my watch, I realized I had to find my sister soon. She was in another building. I stepped outside to call her, and we eventually met up. But I realized I had left my briefcase in the meeting room I had been in earlier. When I returned, there was a gentleman speaking and wrapping up his pitch on the presentation platform as I opened the door. I only heard about the last 10 or 15 seconds of what he said: "...sales trainer in the automobile business. Thank you for listening to my pitch this morning." As I walked in to get my briefcase, he was walking out to leave.

I hurried and got my belongings and stopped him outside and asked if he could expand on what I heard him talking about because I missed it. He went on to explain to me how he had previously worked for a well-known training and consulting company, but he was recently fired. As we shared each other's employment history, he highly recommended that I apply with the company he no longer worked for. He thought it would work out great for me, even though it hadn't ended well for him. Two weeks after speaking to that guy, I was talking to the company's vice president and was hired in days. I've worked for that company for over 17 years, and that guy who recommended me eventually came back and we worked together.

As for the list, it checked every item and even more. My family and I have taken many family trips together from the miles and points that I've racked up over the years, and some of my co-workers are some of my best friends to this day. The point of this story is to show that you can know specifically what you desire, but only God knows the when and the how to get it to you with perfect timing. You can't plan or create timing. You just have to be consistent in your movement and pursuit of what you want. In my case, it was the difference of a matter of seconds, and I could have missed it. But forgetting a briefcase was designed to ensure I didn't. Trust God and His timing. It's something only He can orchestrate. Allow Him by letting go of logic and be diligent in being guided by His promptings and believe that what He has planned for you will absolutely manifest itself, in His timing.

If you've read a lot of self-help and business books like I have, you've probably noticed how everyone's path to success is different, yet some of the challenges they face along the way are similar, especially those rags-to-riches stories. In between the planning and the sacrificial moments of doing everything they could to bring their dreams to a reality, many of them experienced sudden unexpected shifts during their journey that seemed to catapult them in the right direction—a divine moment or epiphany of sorts where they were just about to give up or give in, when something seemed to come together that made everything work out—a lucky break at the right time. Regardless of what you choose to label it, that "something" moment or person could not have been scheduled in a business plan on the climb to success. It just seems to happen.

This is when the forces of spiritual law and the principles of the divine are at work. Without most people's awareness, the belief and faith they started the journey with are the very things that went to work on their behalf from the beginning. But those divine helpers continue to operate only when you're constantly moving in a direction towards what you have believed in. Whether it's an unexpected phone call from someone you've never met or someone you were introduced to long ago, or your lucky numbers, or whatever; it's things that couldn't be put in a business plan for the timing on this day, at this time, with this thing to catapult your business and explode!

DON'T BE ANXIOUS

My wife and I once aspired to start a business. We love entertainment events, weddings, and large family gatherings, so we desired to build and manage an events venue as a family business. We put a well thought-out and impressive business plan together and talked to many banks and business consultants for advice. Everyone thought our vision and ideas were unique and would work considering the massive amount of opportunity the area provided to be successful. We felt great about the feedback and were confident because we did our homework and had everything in place.

But no matter how hard we tried, we ran into roadblock after roadblock when it came to capital for funding the project. We didn't have credit or personal cash issues, but for some reason, banks did not want to move forward with our plans. A few months later, COVID-19 hit the world, and everything shut down. Non-essential businesses like entertainment and wedding venues were hit extremely hard. Looking back, we now understand that had we pushed harder and tried to force or manipulate our dream into a reality, we would have been financially stuck with mountains of debt to pay but with no revenue coming in due to the pandemic.

We were saved from a bad situation all because of "bad" timing that could have worked against us. We had done everything we possibly could to make it happen, but because God knew our hearts and He also knew what was about to affect the entire world in just a few short months, He protected us and would not let it happen at that time. Timing can work in your favor or timing can work against you. In the Bible, Philippians 4:6–7 (CEB) says, "Don't be anxious about anything; rather, bring up all of your requests to God in your prayers and petitions, along with giving thanks. Then the peace of God that exceeds all understanding will keep your hearts and minds safe in Christ Jesus." The tip here is to move when God says move and settle when God says settle.

To demonstrate this point a little further, let's look at what some people would consider a boring piece of scripture. It's a little lengthy, but I highly recommend that you read all of it, because it's a perfect example of how and why God leads His people the way that He does. The passage is Numbers 9:15–23 (CEB): "On the day the dwelling was erected, the cloud covered the dwelling, the covenant tent. At night until morning, the cloud appeared with lightning over the dwelling. It was always there. The cloud covered it by day, appearing with lightning at night. Whenever the cloud ascended from the tent, the Israelites would march. And the Israelites would camp wherever the cloud settled. At the Lord's command, the Israelites would march, and at the Lord's command they would camp. As long as the cloud settled on the dwelling, they would camp. When the cloud lingered on the meeting tent for many days, the Israelites would observe the Lord's direction and they wouldn't march. Sometimes the cloud would be over the dwelling for a number of days, so they would camp at the Lord's command, marching again only at the Lord's command. Sometimes the cloud would settle only overnight, and they would march when the cloud ascended in the morning. Whether it was day or night, they would march when the cloud ascended. Whether it was two days, or a month, or a long time, the Israelites would camp so long as the cloud lingered on the dwelling and settled on it. They wouldn't march. But when it ascended, they would march. They camped at the Lord's command and they marched at the Lord's command. They followed the Lord's direction according to the Lord's command through Moses."

Do you understand the gist of these passages? Loading and unloading all the belongings they had with them during this journey through the desert must have been exhausting. But they only moved when the cloud moved and camped when the cloud settled, regardless of the length of time between each trip. This was clearly done intentionally by God. Notice how the pattern of starting and camping was never for a consistent amount of time, like every three days or every 18 hours. It was different each time. Whether it was days or hours or months, they never knew what or when to camp and unpack or load up and move unless the cloud moved, because God did not want them to go ahead of Him. And He does not want you and me to get ahead of Him either. This is much like walking with God and submitting to His guidance today. He never wants you to think ahead of Him or forecast what He might do next. He never wants you to think ahead of how something should or will happen. As long as you are sensitive and obedient to His prompting, He will lead you to prosperity and a desired end. This way, you will always walk into wealth the right way. The Bible says in Proverbs 10:22 (CEB), "The Lord's blessing makes a person rich and no trouble is added to it."

This is so important because many people I see who are well meaning in their journey towards a wealthy future falter or get off course because they try and make things happen. You can tell they're not listening to the quiet instructions that God has given them because they're anxious and frustrated. It's not just about listening or believing or speaking in faith. It's about humility and obedience to the guidance that God's spirit is speaking to your spirit and walking it out with patience to experience manifestation in your life. Listening to God's prompting and perfect timing, whether it's to move or not to move, is vitally important as you prepare and journey on the way to wealth.

YOUR BRAIN IS A PROCESSOR

If you're like me, you probably don't know much about how the innerworkings of computers operate. While I'm not a gearhead or techno geek, I do enjoy conversations about technology. I understand some of the basics about computer components and how those components function with one another, like the processor, the monitor, the mouse or magic pad, the motherboard, Bluetooth, Wi-Fi, and the On button. I know there's more to it than that, but for me, that's about it.

While once working as director of a recruiting firm, I had to learn a lot about IT and accounting software, because we placed and filled roles for IT and accounting professionals with outside companies. I had to learn the ins and outs of the IT world fast. IT roles, in most cases, are divided into two main areas, the systems network area and the programming area. For example, a network administrator is someone who monitors, supports, and helps troubleshoot a network of many computers across an organization, ensuring they're all operating properly and keeping programs updated. A systems programmer designs or develops code with many different languages that produce software programs and computer commands. Most all digital computer commands are written in what's known in computer science as binary code.

Binary code is based on a binary number system in which there are only two possible states, off and on, usually symbolized by 0 (off) and 1 (on). A binary code signal is a series of electrical pulses that represent numbers, characters, and operations to be performed. A device called a clock sends out regular pulses, and components such as transistors switch on (1) or off (0) to pass or block the pulses.

Much like digital computers, our brains operate in the same way. Our brain processes different electrical impulses from imagery that passes through our five senses. These hundreds of thousands of bits of invisible stimulated information are all processed through our brain to determine what, why, and how we are to do one simple thing: Make a choice. Much like binary code, everything we process is to basically determine what to choose, (yes) or (no), to determine whether we "will do" or "won't do" something, move or not move, I can (on) or I can't (off). If we determine in our minds, *This is a waste of my time* or *There is no way this will work*, or something is impossible, our creative flow begins to shut down and stop processing, or it determines "0."

However, when we choose to believe something is a possibility, even though we may not have a solution to the problem, our brains begin to generate and are still in creative or possibility mode. It determines "1." Thoughts like *Hmmm, how can I make this work?* or *There has to be a way to get this done!* keep the mind stimulated with creative pulses that expands your thinking to dig deeper into your higher consciousness.

To simply be guided or directed by your brain is why so many people make bad choices. No matter what state of mind or position you are in today for your life, good or bad, happy or depressed, it's a collection of choices and decisions that you've made along the way that's gotten you to where you are now. Even as you read these words, you are determining whether to trust what I'm saying or not. By only following the guidance of logic, or feelings of emotions, from your brain or nerve center, you are destined to choose the wrong direction more often than not. Our feelings are fleeting—the way you feel today may be different from the way you'll feel tomorrow.

To make a critical life's decision solely based on emotion or feeling is simply not wise. Quite frankly, our emotions can lie to us. Logic is no different. While making a sensible decision through logic has its place, simple reasoning cannot determine timing. Remember what I said about my wife's and my decision to build a venue? It all made sense to us, but we had no clue a world pandemic was on the horizon. This is why it's so important that we go deeper into ourselves and search our hearts on matters. Our spirit and minds are usually in conflict with one and other. In fact, Galatians 5:17 (NIV) says, "For the flesh desires what is contrary to the Spirit, and the Spirit what is contrary to the flesh. They are in conflict with each other, so that you are not to do whatever you want."

In chapter 1, I stated that your soul is basically your center or your central nature. It's where you choose to either follow your senses or follow your spirit. Your brain is simply processing the information to make the choice. Your senses have their place in decision making, but it's important as you move forward on the path to wealth that you get in tune and learn to listen to your higher self, that is, your spirit paralleled with His spirit, because God has designed you to prosper, and He will guide you into *all* truth and to an expected end result of that you have believed.

BIBLICAL NUMEROLOGY

Since we're talking about decisions, processors, and numbers, we might as well dabble in biblical numerology for a moment. Not Chaldean, Kabbalah, Tamil, Pythagorean, or mystic numerology, but biblical numerology. I'm not going to go too in depth with it, but I encourage you to look it up and study some of it. A good resource I found to be quite intuitive and in depth on this subject is a site called biblestudy.org. If you're reading this on a computer, type in "the meaning of numbers," and you'll get a wealth of information on the topic, including numbers you can click and it will give you a detailed definition and meaning for that given number.[68] Of course, this is only one suggested resource, but I encourage you to do some further exploration of your own. I'm sure you can find several other resources that can help expand your knowledge and understanding of numbers in the Bible.

Numbers can play a very significant role in the way divine laws operate, as well as in some of the ways God's spirit will guide you. The day or the year that you were born or your age all have significant meaning. Again, not like a horoscope but more like the time and seasons. There are a few that I want to point out here because as I'm being led by the spirit, I usually look for certain guidance in numbers, too. As you familiarize yourself with each and learn the meanings behind them, you, too, can know whether or not a certain path is God's direction.

Here are numbers in sequential order and their meaning according to biblical numerology.

---

68 "the meaning of numbers," Bible Study, accessed August 10, 2021, https://www.biblestudy.org/search.php?zoom_query=the+meaning+of+numbers&x=25&y=21&zoom_per_page=7.

NUMBER 1—Oneness, *Life and Unity; New beginnings.* Usually, when there's only one of something, it represents life or unity. There's only one way to be born. There is only one canal to be born through. In your body, the parts that sustain your life consist of one. There's only one heart, one brain, and only one life-giving organ. Notice also that you have one mouth, which can speak words of life or death.

NUMBER 2—Union; Division; Witnessing. The number 2 is usually to co-incide one with the other, as balance in union or to witness and verify. We have two eyes and arms and two legs. If you and I were looking in the sky and we both saw a UFO, if I wasn't sure of what I was looking at and I asked you, "Are you seeing what I'm seeing?" then you can confirm and verify as a witness that we are both looking at the same thing.

NUMBER 3—*Divine completeness.* All of creation is designed in groups of threes. We live in a three-dimensional world. The atmosphere is made up of solids, liquids, and gases. God's character or God's makeup is known as the Trinity: God the Father, God the Son, and God the Holy Spirit. We are made up of mind, body, and spirit. Even the atom and subatomic world is constructed in groups of three. An atom has three constituent parts: protons, neutrons, and electrons.

NUMBER 4—*represents creation, and the world around us.* Seasons come in fours: summer, winter, fall, and spring. We have four ocean basins or main bodies of water on earth—the Atlantic, Pacific, Indian, and Arctic. Geo-graphical directions are composed of north, south, east, and west. Geometric dimensions comprise of height, length, width, and depth.

NUMBER 5—*represents God's goodness, Grace.* The first five books of the New Testament Bible are known as the Pentateuch. If you possess five fingers, five toes, and five main limbs; your torso, legs, and arms; your neck and head, then that's grace. If you work only five days in a week and not six or seven days, that's God's goodness and grace. We have five senses. (Coincidentally, my family is a family of five.)

6—*represents weakness of man; the manifestation of sin; and Satan.*

7—*represents spiritual completeness and perfection.*

8—*sights new beginnings or new order.*

9—*is divine completeness from the Father, or fruit of the spirit.*

10—*is testimony, law, and responsibility.*

11—*shows disorder and judgment.*

12—*is governmental perfection.*

13—*Apostasy; depravity and rebellion.*

14—*Salvation; deliverance.*

15—*is rest.*

16—*is love.*

17—*is victory.*

18—*is bondage.*

19—*is faith.*

20—*is redemption.*

While I only chose to list the meaning of the first 20 numbers, there are many more you can research and define the biblical meaning behind them. Numerous times I've studied numbers while listening to my heart in making decisions. They have always guided or steered me either into the destiny that God had for me, or it steered me completely away from what could have been devastation. Of all the homes we've bought and sold over the years, our favorite had the address with the numbers 3737. As you may have noticed on the chart above, the number three represents divine completeness or perfection, and the number seven represents spiritual completeness. That was the address of a house we owned in a neighborhood where selling it could have been a major challenge, but we sold it within minutes.

EVERYTHING IS CIRCULAR

Like biblical numerology, God plants heavenly principles on earth through time and seasons, too. Time was created and inserted into our atmosphere for several reasons. Time has been described as the indefinite continued progress of existence and events that occurs in an apparently irreversible succession from the past, through the present, into the future. It's a component quantity of various measurements used to sequence events, to compare the duration of events or the intervals between them, and to quantify rates of change in material reality or in the conscious experience. Based on the rotation of the earth, time can be measured by observing celestial bodies. Astronomers found that it was more accurate to establish time by observing stars as they crossed a meridian rather than by observing the position of the sun in the sky.[69]

Seasons are caused by earth's tilted axis.[70] Throughout the year, different parts of earth receive the sun's most direct rays. Therefore, when the North Pole tilts toward the sun, it's summer in the Northern Hemisphere, and when the South Pole tilts toward the sun, it's winter in the Northern Hemisphere. This also helps people in agriculture know when to plant and when to harvest. These two elements combined give us a glimpse into understanding how spiritual laws operate. For instance, everything created by God has been created in a circular motion. If you look at the atom, there are electrons, neutrons, and protons that circle around the atom. From the smallest particles of creation to the farthest galaxies and nebulas, all of it operates in a circular motion.

Seasons rotate in a circular motion, summer, winter, fall, and spring, and then back again to summer. Therefore, the phases of life itself operate in a circular motion—conception, birth, life, and death, and back to life again. We also experience phases within a life span. We start with needing attention for our every need as infants, which is *dependency*. We grow to where we can do some things for ourselves, yet there are some things we may need assistance with. This is *interdependence*. When we are fully grown, we are free to provide and make decisions for ourselves. This is *independence*. As we get older, we may slow down a little. We're back to *interdependency*. As our bodies get older and our motor skills diminish, we come full circle back to *dependency*. This is where most of our elderly cannot operate or function completely on their own without assistance and constant care. Life works in a circular motion,

69   "Keeping Time," Lumen Astronomy, accessed August 10, 2021, https://courses.lumenlearning.com/astronomy/chapter/keeping-time/.

70   "What Causes the Seasons?" NASA Science Space Place, updated July 22, 2021, https://spaceplace.nasa.gov/seasons/en/.

and like the cycle of seasons, it rotates in four or five phases—the numbers for creation and God's grace.

These observations will play a huge role for wealth building as I walk you through the next section of preparation. As you begin to put spiritual law into practice, patience and unwavering belief will be required. You will be putting natural and supernatural law together to work on your behalf. The passage Isaiah 55:11 says that when God speaks, his word never returns back to Him, void or empty.

This means that when you speak, your words will go out as containers to be filled by what you have spoken, launched, and fueled by faith and belief. Whatever is said from the heart will return back to you, manifested based on what it is that you have spoken and believed. This is a very simple truth, yet so many fail in this area. They begin to process in their minds that something did or didn't work too soon, thereby aborting the mission of what has been spoken. By processing and choosing plan B, it says they never truly trusted or believed their plan A. Divine laws have been in place and have existed long before you and I entered the earth. Therefore, if something doesn't work, question yourself, not the divine, to see what it is you must correct.

CHAPTER 12

EXPECT OPPOSITION

"Success is not measured by what you accomplish, but by the opposition you have encountered, and the courage with which you have maintained the struggle against overwhelming odds."

—*Orison Swett Marden*[71]

You've probably heard the saying, "Truth is stranger than fiction." This was said when someone wanted to point out or emphasize that real events are sometimes stranger than imaginary or made-up stories. Like all great stories, they have elements in common that grab the audience's attention: exciting twists, relatable characters, vivid descriptions, and lasting emotional effects. Behind every great story is a strong structure made up of the essential components of storytelling, which are plot, characters, settings, theme, point of view, and tone.

Let's focus on the characters for a moment. A story usually includes several of them, each with a different role or purpose. Regardless of how many characters a story has, however, there is almost always a protagonist and an antagonist. These characters are vital to the development of the story, and the plot usually revolves around them. The protagonist is the main character of

---

71   Orison Swett Marden, *An Iron Will* (Saint Paul, MN: Wilder Publications, 2008).

a story. He or she has a clear goal to accomplish or a conflict to overcome. The antagonists oppose protagonists, standing between them and their ultimate goals. The antagonist can be presented in the form of any person, place, thing, or situation that represents a tremendous obstacle to the protagonist.

Real life is no different. You are the main character in your life's story. And believe me, there are antagonists that opposes all the good you may stand for. The plot of your life's story is to discover your purpose and how you are to use all that you were created to be in an effort to contribute to humanity for the glory of your creator, which can be accomplished in many different ways.

Since the beginning of time, there has been a battle of incredible forces between good and evil, light and darkness, antagonist and protagonist, Satan and God. Regardless of whether you choose to believe if there is or isn't evil or a devil or demons, the truth is, you and I are the chess pieces used to uphold whoever's kingdom or government will reign or fall—the kingdom of light or the kingdom of darkness. We cannot battle demonic forces with our own strength and intelligence. And even though our hearts may be with Christ Jesus, when we succumb to our humanity, life becomes an impossible fight to win apart from the wisdom, power, and guidance of God through His spirit.

Remember the struggles of Doug and Helen I referenced in chapter 2? How, no matter how hard they tried to improve their financial lives and no matter their plans or extra jobs they worked, it never seemed to propel them any further? Those are examples of human effort battling against supernatural forces. Anything that represents God's goodness—marriage, prosperity, health, or wealth—dark forces will attack to keep you from progressing. It is only by God's spirit that you can overcome darkness and evil forces forged against you to achieve your mission on this earth and become completely fulfilled in what you have been created to do. Ephesians 6:12 (NIV) says, "For our struggle is not against flesh and blood, but against the rulers, against the authorities, against the powers of this dark world and against the spiritual forces of evil in the heavenly realms."

Please understand that as you believe in the power of God in you, combined with your super nature, the enemy is not only against you, but wants to destroy you and everything that represents the kingdom of light. To be clear, the enemy hates you, but it's not personal—it's God he hates, because you have been placed above darkness and have been given rule and dominion over it by God himself. You have a power and position of sonship that was freely given to you, a creation that is deemed unworthy and undeserving by the ruler of darkness.

Hebrews 2:6–8 (CEB) says, "Instead, someone declared somewhere, 'What is humanity that you think about them? Or what are the human beings that you care about them? For a while you made them lower than angels. You crowned the human beings with glory and honor. You put everything under their control. *When he puts everything under their control, he doesn't leave anything out of control.*'"

Because of this eternal jealousy, you are enemy number one. Remember, you were made like God, in His image and in His likeness. So, your enemy's plan is to ensure you never discover your true self and you live forever disconnected from your true power source for all eternity, like he does.

THE DEVIL IS IN THE DETAILS

The Bible references him by many names: Deceiver, Accuser, Lord of the Air, Lord of the Flies, Serpent, the Devil, Lucifer, the Prince of Darkness, Prince of Persia, etc. He is a fallen angel that opposed God himself. He was so influential that one-third of Heaven's angels followed him and were cast out of Heaven with him. Where is his prison or destination of exile? Right here in the core of the earth, where man was created to rule over him until final judgment. Revelation 12:9 (NIV) says, "The great dragon was hurled down—that ancient serpent called the devil, or Satan, who leads the whole world astray. He was hurled to the earth, and his angels with him." He opposes *anything* or any order that represents light, love, and the glory of God, which includes God's most prized creation, you and me. Make no mistake, he is alive and very active in the lives of many. Just look at the state of man and the problems we face throughout the world.

When man disobeyed God's order, darkness became the rule of this world. God's divine system of fatherly provision was replaced by a system of sweat and toil for your supply. By this dark order, the enemy's endgame is to build a kingdom that will ultimately destroy all of mankind, starting with the idea that you cannot trust God; therefore, you must trust yourself.

By using evil tactics and dark forces of influence, humans are fueled by the desire to go after and possess temporal things, yet the system makes them very hard to obtain. This endless type of slavery makes man point the finger at God rather than himself or Satan as the reason for life's cruelties. This misplaced trust and unbelief in the character of God cause many to lose focus of eternal things, including their own spirit, which is the DNA of God inside of us. So, man looks inward and begins to trust self, believing he can accomplish anything he desires *without* God, making himself master and god of his own life. It's man's own EGO, which stands for Edging God Out.

Satan is the master of manipulation, and without God's power and guidance to assist you in obtaining wealth, it can be nearly impossible to accomplish, especially for those who claim to be God's own. Satan's goal is to intervene in anything of God and to destroy your and my chances of ever accomplishing our God-given destinies.

However, if you choose not to live for God, by default you become Satan's ally. Don't get it twisted—the enemy promises wealth, fame, and abundance, too. But at a very high cost and by only the means of which he dictates. He gives the illusion of false power by offering the freedom of self-indulgence and self-preservation, but eventually he'll want payment in full for what he gives by demanding self-sacrifice. Make no mistake, the enemy's plan *always* ends in death: dead relationships, dead business, dead awareness of who you are—just death. That's the goal of the kingdom of darkness, to build his kingdom of influence to deceive you and many others.

These old tactics are very effective and can be extremely enticing. He even used them against Jesus himself in Luke 4:5–8 (CEB): "Next the devil led him to a high place and showed him in a single instant all the kingdoms of the world. The devil said, 'I will give you this whole domain and the glory of all these kingdoms. It's been entrusted to me and I can give it to anyone I want. Therefore, if you will worship me, it will all be yours.' Jesus answered, 'It's written, You will worship the Lord your God and serve only him.'"

WHAT'S UP WITH WORSHIP?

To worship is the act of showing respect and love for a god, an excessive admiration for someone.

Worship gives a living entity a power and a posture of superiority like or above God Himself. That's why only He is to be worshiped. As human beings, we are all created to worship. All throughout history man has worshiped something or someone because it is natural to be in awe of something greater than oneself. We hero worship sports and entertainment stars, we idol worship millionaires and billionaires. However, in contrast, we don't typically respect or revere those things that we see as less than or beneath us.

Look at what one of the disciples of Jesus, John, did to an angel who took him to Heaven to give him an insider's look of things that were to come. Pay close attention to the angel's reaction. Revelation 19:9–10 (CEB) says, "Then the angel said to me, 'Write this: Favored are those who have been invited to the wedding banquet of the Lamb.' He said to me, 'These are the true words of God.' Then I fell at his feet to worship him. But he said, 'Don't do that! I'm a servant just like you and your brothers and sisters who hold firmly to the witness of Jesus. Worship God!'"

Clearly, worship is serious stuff, because it is an offering of one's free will, subservient to an entity to do whatever they wish to the one who serves them. The enemy wants to be an imitator of God and wants to be like God but through means of evil and hatred, not love. He is the direct opposite of all that God is. God blesses; he curses. God heals; he inflicts pain and suffering. God encourages; he discourages. God is freedom; he is bondage. He opposes anything God created and upholds as holy, because he was evicted from Heaven because of pride and envy of God himself! Isaiah 14:12–17 (CEB) explains, "How you've fallen from heaven, morning star, son of dawn. You are cut down to earth, helpless on your back! You said to yourself, I will climb up to heaven; above God's stars, I will raise my throne. I'll sit on the mount of assembly, on the heights of Zaphon. I'll go up to the cloud tops; I'll be like the Most High!" And Revelation 12:12 (CEB) says, "Therefore, rejoice, you heavens and you who dwell in them. But oh! The horror for the earth and sea!

The devil has come down to you with great rage, for he knows that he only has a short time."

So, like God, Satan wants to build his kingdom through man, but his purposes are for man's destruction and ultimately his demise. He uses man to turn attention away from God and to himself to destroy mankind before he is eternally destroyed. But he is bound and subject to the same laws that we are. And if you are ignorant to what those laws and rules are to live, then he has every legal right to try and deceive, to come in and wreak havoc on everything you own and represent.

But he has to convince *you* through his influence of your own free will, just like in the garden of Eden since the beginning. The prize is life or death. But the good news is that you must know you are battling with a defeated and beaten opponent. Jesus said in Luke 10:18–19 (NIV), "I saw Satan fall like lightning from heaven. I have given you authority to trample on snakes and scorpions and to overcome ALL the power of the enemy; nothing will harm you." I put ALL in caps for you to demonstrate that NOTHING he can do to you will succeed, but he must convince you otherwise. To defeat him in any situation is as simple as *submitting yourself to God. Resist the devil and he will run from you.*

The only way the enemy can attack you is through your mind, using impulsiveness, fear, excitement, and other emotions to ensure entrance so that you will do exactly what he planned you would do. Like God, he must use people to carry out his will. If he can't get you to carry out his mission directly, then he'll use someone or something else that influences you, indirectly. He and demonic forces are very patient and are working towards long-term results. The bottom line is that we are at war with invisible evil forces of darkness. And the battle is for your soul. Look at what 2 Corinthians 10:3–4 (CEB) says, "Although we live in the world, we don't fight our battles with human methods. Our weapons that we fight with aren't human, but instead they are powered by God for the destruction of fortresses." Spiritual weapons are the only effective way to counter and root out the true cause of poverty and lack in your life. Without identifying your wealth journey as a spiritual one, you are positioning yourself for a lifetime of activity that will, quite frankly, get you no further than you are right now. This kind of thinking is exactly what dark forces are counting on.

SECTION IV: THE WAY TO WEALTH

CHAPTER 13

POSITIONING FOR WEALTH

"True wealth is not of the pocket, but of the heart and of the mind."
—*Kevin Gates*[72]

In chapter 3, I described how I came to know Jesus personally and how He has positively impacted my life to this very day. His presence and love fulfill me in ways words can't adequately express. His glorious effect on my life has permeated throughout my own family as they experience the awesomeness of all that He is and all that He provides. I can say without question that if my life were to end today, I would be at peace knowing where I'm going and comfortable with the life that I have led here on earth. But I also know that's not going to happen anytime soon, as I have so much more to offer to the world before I go.

Hopefully, my experiences and the decisions I made for my life long ago inspire you to want to experience Jesus for yourself. Therefore, before you read any further about the plan I have for building extraordinary wealth for

---

72   Temi Adebowale, "Kevin Gates Says He's Spent About $2.5 Million on Jewelry," *Men's Health*, November 21, 2019, https://www.menshealth.com/entertainment/a29872572/kevin-gates-salary-mens-wealth/.

you and your family's future, it's somewhat inconsequential if you haven't received the power of God inside of you to help bring all of what you want to manifestation.

If you've never heard the plan of salvation for how to receive Jesus into your life, it's simply this: Decide to turn away from the world's way of living and decide to follow and worship Jesus only. Ask him to come into your heart and receive Him as your Lord and Savior. Just say this: "Lord Jesus, I no longer choose to follow the ways of the world, but I'm making my decision now to follow you. Come into my heart and I make *you* my Lord and Savior from this day forward. Fill me with your Holy Spirit as I accept Him now."

That's it. If you were sincere with what you've just said, then welcome to the family of God.

See, to receive Christ into your heart is a free gift. You can't earn or prepare yourself for salvation, because nothing we could ever do would be good enough to make us worthy of it. Therefore, Jesus made it simple and for anyone who believes. Just ask, because the door has already been opened long ago. If you don't know any scriptures in the Bible, John 3:16–17 (CEB) makes it pretty clear: "God so loved the world that he gave his only Son, so that everyone who believes in him won't perish but will have eternal life. God didn't send his Son into the world to judge the world, but that the world might be saved through him."

If you've ever called on Jesus to help you in any situation in your life, guess what? He's entered in. All you have to do now is acknowledge Him as your own and that you belong to Him. Salvation makes life so much easier, because it releases life's pressure from you and puts it on your God. Why carry the burdens of life that are too heavy for you to bear? Cast your cares upon Him, and He will carry the load for you. Besides, you and I don't even know what is going to happen the next five minutes of our lives. For all we know, as you're reading, a vehicle could crash into the room where you are to harm you, or someone could call you wanting to positively change your life financially. My point is, we have no way of planning or knowing what our future is, but the Creator of all does.

FIND A CAUSE

Giving your life to the Lord guarantees you a path to success, provided you follow His guidance. He promises that anything you ask for in His name and according to His will is yours. Some would argue that you should not ask for wealth. In fact, the scriptures say don't seek or run after riches. But if the purpose for your life involves wealth, then shouldn't God provide it? What good employer would ask you to do a task without providing you the tools and resources necessary to accomplish it? So, instead of asking for wealth, ask for a cause, one that speaks to your heart for humanity.

For example, I have a heart for marriages and family in general. I believe the family is the core of society that reflects how everyone around us functions both personally and professionally. Because of my belief, one of my causes is to help restore and encourage married couples to see the union from God's perspective and demonstrate how He wants to use the marital relationship to grow and mature us individually to accomplish His will on earth. I've spent countless hours, days, and even months acquiring my certifications to become a Christian family counselor. As you can probably imagine, this cause has put enormous pressure on my marriage and family relationships. But through all of it, God has provided immeasurably in ways I would have never imagined.

There are tons of causes that God would endorse and provide everything you could ever need to accomplish them. Jesus Himself said the harvest for humanity is ripe and plentiful but the workers to accomplish it are few. People are hurting all over the world, and they are looking for solutions to some of life's most pressing concerns. If you choose to be a solution for victims of sex trafficking, orphans, the homeless, the poor, helping felons who have changed their lives transition into civilian life, helping our veterans, widows, adoptions for parents who long to have children, even helping addicted millionaires get clean; whatever it is, find a cause and get involved. Build something, invent something, create something, but do something. If it helps lift humanity and leads them to reconnect to God, you can guarantee it's God's will. God loves people. All people. And if you're sincere about being a solution through God's spirit, there is nothing that He would hold back from you to accomplish His will on earth.

So, if you haven't already, I highly recommend that you give your life to Jesus and take up a cause. There's no downside to it. You'll have the power to battle the enemy and the Holy Spirit to guide you and provide whatever you could ask for through faith and divine laws. In addition, He'll give you joy and peace in the dark times and will be a light to your feet helping you every step of the way to success. Others without God are searching and looking for answers to life just like I did. Now I point them in His direction, knowing that God is always there, and He will walk them through any problem with every natural and supernatural solution.

I will warn you, though, every day will not be a bed of roses and every day will not be joyous. The life of a believer has its peaks and valleys just like anyone else's. The difference, however, is with the valleys, God uses those times to build the character and the strength you'll need to reach and fulfill your destiny. The downtimes and the valleys can be a very significant, peaceful, joyous, and life-altering touchstone if you humble yourself and submit to His way and not yours.

I've had many dark days and nights in my life. And I can tell you from experience that those were not times I would volunteer for of my own free will. That's why He allows those circumstances to happen because natural behavior would reject them. But I would never trade in those dark times for times of pleasure because they helped shape and mature me for my destiny. Those times helped me trust Him and fall deeply in love with His care for me all over again, knowing that no person can love me as God can.

But those are my experiences. The path to wealth for you will be tailor-made for you and most likely will not be a straight and direct path. Everyone has their way to their destinies, and that's the beauty of life. The experiences that we all get to share are all different from one person to the next. Nevertheless, the journey and the destinations are the same. We are more than conquerors in Jesus, and we have the power to build wealth. It is God's will that you profit and that you be in good health even as your soul prospers.

STAY IN YOUR LANE

If you're wondering what your purpose in life is, have no fear. You're proba-bly walking it out right now. You may be thinking the job you're doing now is some dead-end road to nowhere. You may be working at some fast-food restaurant or sweeping floors somewhere, or you're in an office cubicle with no desire to climb up the corporate ladder, but whether you're a mother or father at home raising your children or working on the back of a sanita-tion truck, it doesn't matter. You have to believe and trust that whatever it is you're doing, those things are necessary for where you're going. Listen to your heart—even if it's something you aspire to do that has nothing to do with what you're currently doing, stay there until you sense God's prompting to do something different.

Every occupation I've had in the past developed and prepared me for where I am today. I also started with odd jobs like anyone else. But during those times, those jobs taught me discipline, how to be loyal, how to be on time, how to deal with tough personalities, and how to stick with something and trust God to guide me and not my impulses. Remember those five pillars of society I spoke of in the previous chapter? They include the areas of financial, legal, entertainment, social, and health.

Regardless of where you are in life right now, you're probably serving in one of those pillars. Learn everything there is to learn in what you're doing. When your heart begins to speak to you about doing something different, bring it before God and prepare to make a shift. I can guarantee you, whatever you're learning now will transfer over to what your desires are in the future. If you're currently serving in the health pillar, for example, but your desires are to be in entertainment, then entertain people in the health sector. That's using your faith.

Many years ago, I had no idea that my communication skills at a car deal-ership were developing me for public speaking and business consulting. I had no desire to sell cars, but the prompting to do so stirred within me and I couldn't get rid of it. Once I embraced the thought of it and began to pursue it, guess what? It was everything I thought it was, and I didn't like it. But I knew that's where I was supposed to be and I decided to stick with it, regardless of how I felt. From that experience, I developed compassion for people who were struggling in their finances. I learned about budgets and people's emotional responses to things and money. I learned how to recognize different personality types and shift my communication approach with them to make them feel more comfortable with me. These skills have taken me all over North America, speaking and training professionals in the areas of sales, communication, and leadership—many of whom I have inspired to be better parents, spouses, sons, and daughters to those they love around them. I've been invited into their homes, sharing the love of God and the discovery of showing them what the higher self can do for them. I had no idea any of this would develop from selling cars on a car dealership's sales floor. But it started from serving in the financial pillar of society working as a teller at a bank.

Here's the short version of that story. My wife and I wanted a new car because our new jobs required traveling further, and the new distance began to take its toll on our older vehicles. Honda had just created a new luxury division in America called Acura. Not many people had heard of it at the time and that's the vehicle we bought. That vehicle started quite a few conversations at grocery stores and gas stations. Every time someone asked me about our car, I found myself giving a 10-point walk-around presentation describing key features and how much we enjoyed it. I would get so enthralled in conversations with people when they'd ask that sometimes I'd forget my wife was sitting in the car waiting to leave. When I would get inside, she would look at me with this "Really?" look and say, "If you're going to talk this much about the car, you might as well sell them for a living." Those spoken words started the prompting inside me.

Along with those spoken words, sometime later I helped a friend who was struggling with a need for transportation buy a car. Like an agent, I expedited all the paperwork that needed signing back and forth between the dealership and my friend, because he worked two jobs and could never get away. So, I decided to do this, wanting to prove to him that buying a car was easy.

The person who sold the vehicle was so impressed with my willingness to help a friend that he suggested I try selling cars as a career. I politely told him that wasn't for me, but something inside me knew this was the direction to go.

After some time, and a lot of prompting from God's spirit, I pursued it and lo and behold, the door was open. Well, to be honest, it took a while because I went to every other car dealership except the one that God told me to go to in the beginning. So, instead of a direct line with no time wasted to where I should have been, it took me six months of rejection from others to finally go to where He wanted me to be all along. I was hired in two days and before you know it, I was starting my new career as a new car sales professional.

GOD'S WEALTH PLAN

Before I share with you a structure of how to plan and position your finances to receive wealth, you first must commit your life to getting out of financial debt. No matter the plan, the one I'm about to lay out or some other, if you have a love affair with financial debt, then you're not going to be wealthy, ever.

I know people who live with tons of debt, and they don't seem to mind it one bit. Yet, those same people are the ones who have no downtime because they are always working, and they can't help others with anything because they are barely getting by themselves. If you're in debt even a little and you're ok with it, this mindset has to change. You have to start somewhere, so I'll give you this to consider if you're not afraid of a little hard work and self-discipline:

- Get out of debt on your own or with professional help.

- Aspire to achieve the kind of financial stability that most people never accomplish.

- Commit to helping others do the same.

Start with the natural way of eliminating your debt, and God will intervene with the divine and supernatural way to wealth as you progress. Show Him you are serious about following His plan of abundance and supply by first showing Him you can be disciplined with His resources. I am neither a licensed money manager nor financial broker, but my wife and I have submitted ourselves to many faith-based personal financial conferences and have even gone through personal finance training to become certified teachers with the Larry Burkett Christian Financial Concepts council while living in California many years ago. There are several ways to get started and many resources you can find online or within churches or other nonprofits that focus on personal finances and how to eliminate financial debt. Here are a few tips I highly recommend to help you get started and on your way to financial freedom.

Make a written plan — writing down your goals will help give you a visible objective from which you can begin to work towards. Some may call it a budget. Regardless of the label, start where you can get your finances in front of you so that you can see clearly what's actually coming in, what's going out, and where it is going. Begin to use what I call a *Penny Diary* to track all the little expenses that seem to go unnoticed throughout a given month. It's simple. Carry around a little 4 x 6 note pad with you every day, or if you're disciplined, make notes of the amounts you spend in the Notes section of your smartphone if you have it. For every small amount you spend, like tips, gum, coffee, tolls, or when you feel compelled to let someone "keep the change," jot it down in your diary. No need to record regular monthly expenses for this one. I recommend doing this for at least one month. You'll be surprised to discover how much you're spending and where it's going. Once you've completed this little exercise, begin to make your plans compatible with God's will, starting with demonstrating your commitment to being a good manager of the resources you've already been given. Learn what your role is from God's perspective.

Commit to God's portion first — I touched on this in chapter 10 when describing the Law of Honor. This principle is a critical and essential element in any financial plan. Honor God by giving at least 10% of what you bring home from your income, which is called tithing. The enemy will fight you on this in the beginning, but I can certainly attest through my own personal experiences, honoring God through giving tithes has helped stretch our finances in ways I can't fully explain. Just trust God when He says in Malachi 3:10 (NIV), "Bring the whole tithe into the storehouse, that there may be food in my house. Test me in this," says the Lord Almighty, "and see if I will not throw open the floodgates of heaven and pour out so much blessing that there will not be room enough to store it."

Reduce or eliminate the use of credit cards — I understand how in some families the total elimination of credit buying may not be feasible. But every family can at least reduce the need for using them. Placing a freeze or putting a dead stop on the use of credit cards is the start of getting yourselves free from financial bondage.

Start eating in more, not out — listen, I love eating out. I admit it. I would eat out every day of my life if I could. But I also know that while I'm enjoying the freedom of not having my wife or myself cook, there's a lot of money that could be a huge savings for you and your family if you simply bought groceries and cooked at home. See how much you'll save in the first month by cooking at home. As you get your expenses under control, perhaps you can ease back into an occasional outing rather than it being the norm.

Budget for groceries online — make a list and stick with it. No impulse items. I order my groceries online and then pick them up curbside at our local store. If this is an option for you, it's a great way to manage the items you need and not be tempted to stray when impulse items are not there to see and purchase in front of you.

Start praying about every expenditure — doing this brings God directly into your life and strengthens your faith so that you can trust Him in greater things—you'll find no purchase is too large or too small to pray about. Bring your whole family in on the petition before God and allow them to share in the spiritual blessing to learn to discern God's will. In the area of new purchases, God may not grant your every wish because often we ask for things that will ultimately hurt us. For practice, consider two future prospective purchases and pray about them before buying.

Set your own goals — when some people allow others to establish their plans and goals, trust me, they're not going to be happy. Unfortunately, this happens quite often. It's a case of when someone begins to feel guilty because of their less *worldly* goals, which can cause others to change their own given course. On the other hand, a person could get involved in investments or get-rich-quick schemes because others around them seem more successful. Remember, God has a plan for your life and your neighbor does not.

Consider starting a side business — believe it or not, starting a business today is now easier than ever before, mainly because of the information age and the ease of use with technology. If you have a skill or a passion for making things, you can sell your products online. I highly recommend talking to others who may be doing something you think you would enjoy. Many major corporations we see today have started in someone's garage. Seek God and listen to your heart. Your answers to financial freedom could have been stored inside of you all along.

Find an extra job — don't think you have the discipline to start your own business? Then consider becoming a driver for Lyft or Uber. Remember that the goal here is to eliminate debt, and it doesn't mean that you'll have to work the extra job forever. Show God that you're serious, and He will magnify the small areas and make them large.

Next, consider this simple way of positioning your finances to receive wealth by creating buckets, or accounts, that allow you to separate and prioritize your income for the future. All you have to do is commit to putting the plan in place and from your heart and commit to walking it out as best you can with God's guidance.

As I said in chapter 12, expect opposition. But don't lose focus and decide to scrap the idea all together. As long as you understand that opposition comes against you because you are breaking barriers, world habits, and strongholds within yourself and in the spirit realm, you can look to God for guidance, and He will assist you. This involves listening to your higher self and not your base nature, which I'll cover in a little bit. You have the power of the Creator of the universe on your side. He'll guide you into ways of experiencing money windfalls—chunks of opportunities, favors, divine connections with people, and so on—to help expedite the plan in record time. Remember the HOV lane during traffic? Yes, like that.

This is not something that I've practiced once and then decided to write about it; this is my family's and my way of living. I've taught my children, close friends, and anyone interested in wanting to impact society positively for the kingdom of God. Those who have followed the plan have experienced tremendous results because we're simply putting divine laws to work. I showed the natural way for debt cancelation; now let's look at the supernatural way of how to position your finances for building wealth.

THE FIVE BUCKETS

Craig Hill, author of the book *Five Wealth Secrets*, once talked about a simple traditional Jewish method of how to separate your finances in preparation for producing wealth.[73] First, consider breaking up your finances into five segments by designating funds for separate priorities: honoring, savings, giving, short-term and long-term investing, and spending and purchasing whatever you want. Each segment is to be separated from the other and broken up into percentages from all your income, as shown in the graphic.

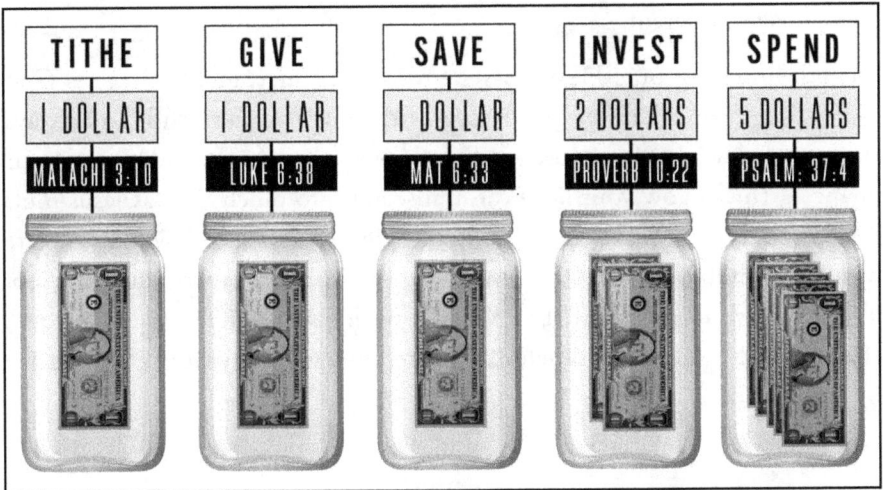

TITHE	GIVE	SAVE	INVEST	SPEND
1 DOLLAR	1 DOLLAR	1 DOLLAR	2 DOLLARS	5 DOLLARS
MALACHI 3:10	LUKE 6:38	MAT 6:33	PROVERB 10:22	PSALM: 37:4

For every 10 dollars, designate:

> 10% Honoring, 10% Giving, 10% Saving, 20% Investing, and 50% for Spending

HONORING

Malachi 3:10–11 (The Message, or MSG) says, "Bring your full tithe to the Temple treasury so there will be ample provisions in my Temple. Test me in this and see if I don't open up heaven itself to you and pour out blessings be-

---

73   Craig Hill, *Five Wealth Secrets 96% of Us Don't Know* (Littleton, CO: Family Foundations International, 2012).

yond your wildest dreams. For my part, I will defend you against marauders [robbers], protect your wheat fields and vegetable gardens against plunderers [looters]."

Honoring is tithing or giving a tenth. Honoring demonstrates to God that you trust the kingdom of God for your provision and means of supply rather than the world's system. By honoring God first, we show that He is first in our lives and before *everything*. This serves two purposes. First, doing this shows whose kingdom you trust, the kingdom of light or the kingdom of darkness. As citizens of Heaven, we honor God just as we pay taxes in this country. Taxes allow us to enjoy certain privileges supplied by the government, such as parks, libraries, roads, and police, fire, and military protection. Heaven is no different.

Second, honoring puts Heaven's system to work in your life. It gives God permission to do whatever He chooses with your finances. And God always chooses to bless, that is, to speak positively over, to multiply, and protect your finances. This is how your little can transcend into much, just as Jesus multiplied the fish and loaves. He simply put Heaven's system to work. If you're wondering exactly what 10% of your income is: If you're working on a job, it's 10% of your gross pay. If you own a business, it's 10% of your income after expenses. Honor God before you use money for anything else, and He will honor you in return.

GIVING

Luke 6:38 (AMP) says, "Give, and it will be given to you. They will pour into your lap a good measure—pressed down, shaken together, and running over [with no space for more]. For with the standard of measurement you use [when you do good to others], it will be measured to you in return."

Giving is the law of the Kingdom of God because the posture of giving is an act of release. When we release, it puts us in a position to receive. Like your hand, your heart has to be open in order to give and also to receive. In God's economy, giving *always* comes back multiplied. It's the law of reciprocity. So be generous, but with wisdom. Having resources set aside specifically for giving allows you to give freely without expecting someone to pay you back, one of the best signs that shows others you are wealthy.

SAVING

Matthew 6:33 (MSG) explains, "Steep your life in God-reality, God-initiative, God-provisions. Don't worry about missing out. You'll find all your everyday human concerns will be met."

Saving money is important because it helps protect you in the event of a financial emergency. Additionally, saving money can help you pay for large purchases, avoid debt, reduce your financial stress, leave a financial legacy, and provide you with a greater sense of financial freedom. God wants you supplied for in every way. But if we gave only, then what would be the benefit of receiving? Regardless of what you are saving for, God wants you to have it. Like children, it pleases Him when we are pleased, and He knows we need and desire things.

INVESTING

Proverbs 10:22 (NIV) tells us, "The blessing of the Lord brings wealth, without painful toil for it." Investing is very wise. Investing is an effective way to put your money to work and build wealth. Smart investing may allow your money to outpace inflation and increase in value. The greater growth potential of investing is primarily due to the power of compounding. A wise investor is patient and will only invest in something that will render a risk-return trade-off on the investment. Let the Holy Spirit guide you in this. Your return will be far greater and so much faster than by natural means.

SPENDING

Psalms 37:4 (NIV) says, "Take delight in the Lord, and he will give you the desires of your heart." Buy *whatever* you want with your spending bucket. This is the will of God! Religion says to be modest for it displays some posture of humility. Yet, we serve an extravagant and lavish God! I love showering my wife with luxury items, mainly because she wouldn't buy them for herself. It shows her and others around her that she is loved and greatly cared for. If your surplus can afford it, then enjoy your spending, as long as it does not rob the other allotted buckets of your finances. Live where you want, drive what you want, and vacation where you want as often as you like. Life is meant to be enjoyed. When we're helping others, we help ourselves. This is the financial freedom we have in God.

CHAPTER 14

PARTNERING WITH THE DIVINE

*"If you're too big to do the small things, then you're too small
to do the big things."*

—*Anonymous*

In chapter 11, I discussed the brain, binary code and how the brain processes information through imagery of the five senses. All this information is designed to allow you to do one thing of your free will, and that is to make a choice with the information you've been given—to agree or disagree, to do or not to do, to say yes or no, to choose or not to choose. In other words, 0s or 1s. All of it is designed to make decisions. Everything you are right now, whether your current situation is good or bad, is a multitude of decisions that have been made based on circumstances, events, people, relationships, and things you've come across in your past through your decision making.

The way you think is based on the way you process information. Whether you are happy or fulfilled in your current state is solely based on a series of decisions you've made in the past. And the way you've processed those past decisions has brought you to where you are now.

If you continue to process information the same way you always have and continue to make the same decisions the same way, then your future will be no different than your current state, because you have not changed your way of thinking, nor have you changed the way you process information when it is presented to you. When you partner with God for wealth, He's going to challenge your thinking and the way you process information. The expanded version of the text of Romans 12:2 (AMP) says, "And do not be conformed to this world [any longer with its superficial values and customs], but be transformed and progressively changed [as you mature spiritually] by the renewing of your mind [focusing on godly values and ethical attitudes], so that you may prove [for yourselves] what the will of God is, that which is good and acceptable and perfect [in His plan and purpose for you]."

Notice at the end it says, "for you." Everything God does is for *you*, not Him. Therefore, you have to bring your thinking up to God's way of thinking, not your current lower-self way of thinking. If you continue processing and choosing the way you always have, then you will continue to get what you've always gotten. Partnering with God requires that you submit yourself to His way and His will, trusting that He will get you exactly what and where you desire. And if you truly know and trust His order of how He does things, then you can bank on the fact that you'll receive more than you asked for or desired. Follow His direction to God levels of wealth. You are now in the God class of society, so think like Him, not based on your understanding but trusting Him based on the character of who He is.

FOLLOWING GOD'S GUIDANCE

To be effective in your life's mission you *must* be led by the Spirit of God, the Holy Spirit. It's by His guidance that we are able to speak with confidence and perform the truly extraordinary exploits of the divine self. Only by His Spirit can you experience true joy, victory, and lasting success *every time*. But to be led by the spirit, you must humble yourself daily and know when it's God's leading and not your own impulses. The best way to discover when God is leading you is to first know how God does *not* lead you.

Looking for signs. Signs can be very misleading in your journey to wealth. The Bible says that signs are to follow you as proof that God is in you and guiding you, not follow signs. Look at Matthew 12:38–39 (CEB): "At that time some of the legal experts and the Pharisees requested of Jesus, 'Teacher, we would like to see a sign from you.' But he replied, 'An evil and unfaithful generation searches for a sign, but it won't receive any sign except Jonah's sign.'"

He was clearly offended. Why? Some people seek after signs and wonders because they do not believe the signs and wonders that have already been performed. Furthermore, signs are to accompany and follow after you as proof you are not operating as everyone else, as being led by your base nature, not you following signs. Mark 16:17–18 (CEB) explains, "These signs will be associated with those who **believe** they will throw out demons in my name. They will speak in new languages. They will pick up snakes with their hands. If they drink anything poisonous, it will not hurt them. They will place their hands on the sick, and they will get well."

Natural instincts. Instincts are the ability of an animal to perform a particular behavior in response to a given stimulus. In other words, an instinctive behavior does not have to be learned or practiced. Animals maintain their entire existence based on natural instincts as a way of survival. However, you and I are not animals. Yet, you see people, even believers, follow their own natural instincts. This type of behavior is genetically hardwired in us. It's an instinct that enhances our ability to cope with environmental incidents, like fear of snakes or the dark. To receive from God and to walk in Him, you are to work in collaboration with God, which are your divine instincts. Jude 1:18–21 (NIV) explains, "In the last times there will be scoffers who will follow their own ungodly desires. These are the people who divide you, who follow mere natural instincts and do not have the Spirit. But you, dear friends, by building yourselves up in your most holy faith and praying in the Holy Spirit, keep yourselves in God's love…" Don't follow your base nature instincts; that's for people who don't know God.

Anxiousness or impulsiveness. From making hasty decisions to getting into fights, impulsivity can cause harm to yourself and those around you. In addition to undermining relationships and your overall sense of well-being, impulsive behaviors can also lead to financial and legal harm if left unchecked. Philippians 4:6 (NIV) says, "Do not be anxious about anything, but in every situation, by prayer and petition, with thanksgiving, present your requests to God."

Being double-minded. Second-guessing too many of your decisions can lead to a sense of anxiety, and it can halt your ability to assert yourself with confidence. This is one of the main ingredients for developing a consciousness of insecurity. In James 1:5–8 (NIV), it says, "If any of you lacks wisdom, you should ask God, who gives generously to all without finding fault, and it will be given to you. But when you ask, you must believe and not doubt, because the one who doubts is like a wave of the sea, blown and tossed by the wind. That person should not expect to receive anything from the Lord. Such a person is double-minded and unstable in all they do." In other words, until you are specific in knowing what you want, your words can't perform the request, and neither can God.

FEAR. It is one of the most effective tactics of the enemy. If dark forces can get you in fear, then your mind will jump ahead into future speculation and deceive you into thinking how circumstances or someone might react as if it has happened already. Fear and impulsions can work hand in hand with one another. To combat fear, remember this acronym: FEAR, or False Evidence Appearing Real. What you convince yourself to believe about a negative person or situation is hardly ever quite what it seems. Usually, behind the veil of fear lies a solution or breakthrough for your problem. Don't buy into fear. Instead, face your fears. The book of 2 Timothy 1:7 (AMP) says, "For God did not give us a spirit of timidity or cowardice or fear, but [He has given us a spirit] of power and of love and of sound judgment and personal discipline [abilities that result in a calm, well-balanced mind and self-control]." Again, our spirit wars or battles against our lower selves. So we must be sensitive to God's prompting or nudging within us and be willing to do and say the things that He tells us.

As you grow in your walk with God's spirit, you'll find in most cases, what He ask of us to do or say may not make sense to our natural mind. To be sure that you are hearing from God, you must *submit* yourself to Him daily and search within yourself to sense His peace. It's His calm and peace He'll give you as guidance in all situations.

The meaning of the word: (submission) **sub·mis·sion** – the action or fact of accepting or yielding to a superior force or to the will or authority of another person. This word is actually two words combined. The "sub" means under, like submarine or subterranean. The word "mission" means a specific task with which a person or group is charged. So, to submit to God means you are under His mission for you, not under your mission. If you knew how to bring health, abundance, or wealth into your life, you probably would have done so by now. In fact, God will not intervene if you feel you have control of your life. I've made enough mistakes to fill a galaxy twice, so I'm tapped out of trying to lead my own life.

Now that we've made a very small list of ways God does not lead us, let's look at ways in which he does.

INNER PEACE

One of the most assured promptings that you are on the right track is that God's peace is always present as your confirmation *after* you have done what He told you, not before. His peace within you is a signal that you have submitted to His will and not your own. It's a position of surrender. Remember, your flesh and mind fight against your spirit. So, when you submit, peace enters in because you are now in sync with God's spirit. Peace is your guardian and your guide.

> Romans 15:13 (NIV): "May the God of hope fill you with all joy and peace in faith so that you overflow with hope by the power of the Holy Spirit."

> 1 Corinthians 14:33 (NIV): "For God is not a God of disorder but of peace..."

> Philippians 4:7 (NIV): "And the peace of God, which transcends all understanding, will guard your hearts and your minds in Christ Jesus."

INWARD WITNESS

Inward witness is also known as conviction. By now you understand that God will make His home inside you, His spirit with your spirit. Inward witness is simply God verifying within your gut that something is not right or what you did was not right. It's the foundation of morality within all of us that checks us to know the difference between right and wrong. When you sense the spirit's prompting for course-correction, don't ignore it. Too often people convince themselves that they are too far gone, or God will never forgive them. Neither is true. Swallow your pride, turn around, and apologize or whatever is necessary to stay on the right course. Your destiny is too valuable to let "saving face" impede or destroy your progress.

> 1 Corinthians 3:16 (CEB): "Don't you know that you are God's temple and God's Spirit lives in you?"

> John 14:23 (NIV): "Jesus replied, 'Anyone who loves me will obey my teaching. My Father will love them, and we will come to them and make our home with them.'"

INWARD VOICE

This is God's preferred and primary way of guiding you to your desired end. Much like the inward witness, you should get familiar with His inward voice. Like your conscience, God speaks to you in ways you can understand. Oftentimes people ask, "How do I know it's God?" Well, He sounds like you, after all, He gave you your voice and He'll never say anything apart or different from His written word.

> John 10:27 (AMP): "The sheep that are My own hear My voice and listen to Me; I know them, and they follow Me."

> Acts 13:2 (NIV): "While they were worshiping the Lord and fasting, the **Holy Spirit said**, 'Set apart for me Barnabas and Saul for the work to which I have called them.'"

ANGELS

In short, angels are the messengers of God. They are sent to mankind to deliver messages, minister to humanity, teach doctrines of salvation, call mankind to repentance, give priesthood keys, save individuals in perilous times, and guide humankind. Oftentimes, they transition to look like regular people when visiting the earth. I've personally encountered three angels in my lifetime.

Acts 8:26 and 29 (NIV): "Now an **angel of the Lord said** to Philip, 'Go south to the road—the desert road—that goes down from Jerusalem to Gaza.' Later as he went, The **Spirit told** Philip, 'Go to that chariot and stay near it.'"

Hebrews 1:14 (NIV): "Are not all angels ministering spirits sent to serve those who will inherit salvation?"

Hebrews 13:2 (NIV): "Do not forget to show hospitality to strangers, for by so doing some people have shown hospitality to angels without knowing it."

PEOPLE: PASTORS, MINISTERS, AND TEACHERS

Have you ever heard a sermon and felt that the minister was speaking directly to you? Have you ever spoken to a stranger, and they gave you advice or something you needed without your asking for it? Yes, God speaks through people. And for those who have dedicated their lives to training themselves to walk with God daily, you would be wise to learn from them.

James 1:22 (NIV): "Do not merely listen to the word, and so deceive yourselves. Do what it says."

Romans 10:17 (AMP): "So faith comes from hearing [what is told], and what is heard comes by the [preaching of the] message concerning Christ."

THE HOLY SCRIPTURES

God's will for your life can always be verified in the scriptures, His word. But you won't know His will if you don't read and listen to His word. If you don't read and listen to His word, then you won't know what He said in His word. And if you don't know what He said in His word, then you can't repeat what He said. If you can't repeat what He said, then you can't know if what He said will actually work. You can only know what He said will work when you are willing to work the words He said. Therefore, you must *read the word of God for yourself.*

2 Peter 1:20-21 (NIV); "Above all, you must understand that no prophecy of Scripture came about by the prophet's own interpretation

of things. For prophecy never had its origin in the human will, but prophets, though human, spoke from God as they were carried along by the Holy Spirit."

2 Timothy 3:16 (NIV); "All Scripture is God-breathed and is useful for teaching, rebuking, correcting and training in righteousness,…"

SEVEN STEPS TO MANIFESTATION

The joys of experiencing the divine at work are when you desire something, and you see exactly what you wanted to manifest into your life. Even better, in most cases, you'll get more than what you've asked for simply because you trusted God with all of your heart, knowing He loves you like His own child, because you are. *So dream big and ask big!*

Jesus made this abundantly clear to those who will simply take Him at his word and believe. The book of Mark records Him as saying this, "Have faith in God [constantly]. I assure you and most solemnly say to you, whoever says to this mountain, 'Be lifted up and thrown into the sea!' and does not doubt in his heart [in God's unlimited power] but believes that what he says is going to take place, it will be done for him [in accordance with God's will]. For this reason, I am telling you, whatever things you ask for in prayer [in accordance with God's will], believe [with confident trust] that you have received them, and they will be given to you."

To put his words into practice, I'm going to describe to you the seven steps necessary to bring what you desire into manifestation or to reality into this dimension.

Step 1: Know **what** you want and **why** you want it. Be specific or definite about it and get God's word on it or get a word from God—by way of inward witness, inward voice, an angel, or through his people. Fixate in your heart, that is your higher self, your spirit, and not your head, the light and truth of the scriptures. Be ready to use God's word against any form of darkness because they will challenge your faith and expectations. Keep in mind, God's answer to prayer and his promises is *always yes.*

2 Corinthians 1:20 (AMP): "For as many as are the promises of God, in Christ they are [all answered] 'Yes.' So through Him we say our 'Amen' to the glory of God."

Step 2: When you ask God for the things that you want, believe that you have already received them *when you pray.* When the Bible says you can have or do something, you can! You must see yourself with it or doing it within your spirit. Experience the emotions and the joy of whatever it is as you envision it within yourself.

1 John 5:14–15 (NIV): "This is the confidence we have in approaching God: that if we ask anything according to his will, he hears us. And if we know that he hears us—whatever we ask—we know that we have what we asked of him."

Step 3: Use your heavenly currency, your faith. Let your every thought and desire affirm that you have what you have asked for. Never let failure or the thought of not having what you've desired enter your mind. Failure and doubt are not options. Doubt is a fiery arrow from the enemies of darkness. Eradicate every vision, dream, feeling, image, idea, and thought that does not fall in line with what you have believed. If God said it, that settles it!

Philippians 4:6–7 (NIV): "Do not be anxious about anything, but in every situation, by prayer and petition, with thanksgiving, present your requests to God. And the peace of God, which transcends all understanding, will guard your hearts and your minds in Christ Jesus."

Isaiah 55:10–11 (NIV): [God says] "As the rain and the snow come down from heaven, and do not return to it without watering the earth and making it bud and flourish, so that it yields seed for the sower and bread for the eater, so is my word that goes out from my mouth: It will not return to me empty but will accomplish what I desire and achieve the purpose for which I sent it."

Step 4: Guard against every evil thought that enters the soul realm, or your mind. Your thought life controls your life. What you think and how you process information is a direct reflection of what is in your spirit. What you are thinking will ultimately affect what comes out of your mouth. Remember, your words are the containers that seek and fulfill what you have spoken. So, what you speak will affect and impact what you manifest into your life.

> Proverbs 18:21 (NIV): "The tongue has the power of life and death, and those who love it will eat its fruit."

> 1 Peter 5:8–9 (AMP): "Be sober [well balanced and self-disciplined], be alert and cautious at all times. That enemy of yours, the devil, prowls around like a roaring lion [fiercely hungry], seeking someone to devour. But resist him, be firm in your faith [against his attack—rooted, established, immovable], knowing that the same experiences of suffering are being experienced by your brothers and sisters throughout the world [you do not suffer alone]."

> James 4:7 (NIV): "Submit yourselves, then, to God. Resist the devil, and he will flee from you."

> 1 John 4:1–3 (NIV): "Dear friends, do not believe every spirit, but test the spirits to see whether they are from God, because many false prophets have gone out into the world. This is how you can recognize the Spirit of God: Every spirit that acknowledges that Jesus Christ has come in the flesh is from God, but every spirit that does not acknowledge Jesus is not from God."

Step 5: Meditate always with scripture on the things you want. I recommend doing this first thing in the morning before any thoughts or suggestions from work, the news, or someone you know influence your thinking. You are basing your answer to your request on what God has said. The word of God is the will of God. See yourself with what you have asked for and with anticipation.

> Proverbs 4:20–22 (AMP): "My son, pay attention to my words and be willing to learn; Open your ears to my sayings. Do not let them escape from your sight; Keep them in the center of your heart. For they are life to those who find them. And healing and health to all their flesh."

> Joshua 1:8 (NIV): "Keep this Book of the law always on your lips; meditate on it day and night, so that you may be careful to do everything written in it. Then you will be prosperous and successful."

Step 6: Make every prayer a statement of fact and faith instead of unbelief. As you develop a consciousness of speaking a declaration as a definitive statement of your faith, it will work hand in hand with your request in the prayer of faith.

> James 5:14–16 (NIV): "Is anyone among you sick? Let them call the elders of the church to pray over them and anoint them with oil in the name of the Lord. And the prayer offered in faith will make the sick person well; the Lord will raise them up. If they have sinned, they will be forgiven. Therefore, confess your sins to each other and pray for each other so that you may be healed. The prayer of a righteous person is powerful and effective."

Step 7: At every opportunity, think about the goodness and the greatness of our God in gratitude and express thanks. No matter where you are in life, there is plenty to be thankful for. If you're reading this book, then that means you have eyesight and understanding. Thank Him for that. His peace will fill your spirit and that will be your confirmation that your request is on its way. All things are possible to the believer! So, give God *praise* before the manifestation of what you have believed for enters this dimensional realm.

> 1 Thessalonians 5:16–23 (CEB): "Rejoice always. Pray continually. Give thanks in every situation because this is God's will for you in Christ Jesus. Don't suppress the Spirit. Don't brush off Spirit-inspired messages but examine everything carefully and hang on to what is good. Avoid every kind of evil. Now, may the God of peace himself cause you to be completely dedicated to him; and may your spirit, soul, and body be kept intact..."

God loves our fellowship. He enjoys our company, but He revels and delights in our praise! Prayer moves the angels of God to work on our behalf, but praise moves the power of God through our faith! Remember those stories of the people who claimed to have died, saw Heaven, and came back to life on the earth? Many of them said they heard singing and music there. Praise is the picture and activity of Heaven!

Imagine if someone wrote a song about you. Let's say that song became number one on the music charts. It's being played all over the country or the world! Let's title it: "The Reasons Why I Love 'Put Your Name Here.'" Do you think people would start to wonder, *who is that person in the song? Is he or she like the song says?* If the song was about you, would it encourage you to want to make good or live up to what they were singing about? This is why churches sing praises before they hear God's message. They know that praise readies the heart and mind to align with the Holy Spirit in us, so that when the word is preached, they are ready to receive the word by faith with thanksgiving!

Prayer and praise together empower us and embolden God. When we are fearful, prayer and praise chase away fear and give us power! When we feel desperate, prayer and praise insulate us with God's peace. When we feel weak and doubtful, prayer and praise encourage us. When we feel burdened and weighed down, prayer and praise lift our burdens off of us. Prayer and praise strengthen our walk as we receive evidence of what we have spoken has come to pass in our life! They build our trust in God and His word even in our sufferings because we know that we will not be put to shame.

SHOW ME THE MONEY

Put your faith into action. *Act on what you say and believe by faith.* Faith is not just saying, but it's both saying and doing. Your level of faith and obedience to doing what God is guiding you through will determine how quickly things happen. James 2:18 (CEB) says, "Someone might claim, 'You have faith and I have action.' But how can I see your faith apart from your actions? Instead, I'll show you my faith by putting it into practice in faithful action." However, I must warn you. There will be times when you can't act simply based on how you feel. There could very well be instructions from the Holy Spirit that will go against or beyond what you are used to. So, prepare to get comfortable being uncomfortable. Hesitation and second-guessing are normal reactions to growth and change. But don't let those impulses stop you from doing or saying what's necessary to bring your desires to manifestation.

If what you desire requires money, then *give* money to receive what it is you are believing for. When you give money, for instance, speak over it and call it what you want before you offer it so that when it is released, it will multiply whatever you called it to be during the exchange process in the kingdom.

When your words and deeds transfer in the kingdom of God, they come back to you based on the law of reciprocity, and it will be multiplied by what you've given. Remember the neighbor's pet story with my daughter? Yes, it works like that.

Furthermore, don't speak facts about what you see in your life; instead, you must speak the truth about what God has said over the facts of what you see in your life. If you don't have the money for something, don't say or tell people you don't have the money. Just say, "Thank you, Lord, for giving [that thing] to me according to your word." Remember what you've asked for and believe you have received it, because God's own words are the only words He trusts.

INVEST IN GOD'S PRODUCTS

Like a seed sown in the earth, it must be planted in good soil. Your heart is the soil where seeds flourish. Do you have a heart (soil) of love, grace, and mercy or one of greed, anger, selfishness, and bitterness? Good soil will nourish your seeds of faith, but negative emotions and thoughts of darkness can kill them. Negative emotions arise from the lower self, and they are designed to block or impede your spirit-filled words from fulfilling what you want. Like shooting holes in a bucket, they cannot hold what's filled inside. Get rid of negative emotions like anger, envy, strife, jealousy, and an overall victim's attitude. If you've offended someone or someone has offended you, apologize or forgive them and move on. What you are hoping for is too important to let evil weapons against you take root and stifle the progress of your manifestation.

Where you plant your seed must be in good soil. Matthew 12:35 (NIV) says, "A good man brings good things out of the good stored up in him, and an evil man brings evil things out of the evil stored up in him." And James 4:3 (AMPC) says, "[Or] you do ask [God for them] and yet fail to receive because you ask with wrong purpose and evil, selfish motives. Your intention is [when you get what you desire] to spend it in sensual pleasures." So, plant where God says plant with the right motives, and you will reap a *great* harvest! If you're not sure where to plant, consider some of God's greatest returns on investment.

THE POOR

Luke 11:41(NIV): "But now as for what is inside you—be generous to the poor, and everything will be clean for you."

Matthew 25:34–40 (NIV): "Then the king will say to those on his right, 'Come, you who will receive good things from my Father. Inherit the kingdom that was prepared for you before the world began. I was hungry and you gave me food to eat. I was thirsty and you gave me a drink. I was a stranger and you welcomed me. I was naked and you gave me clothes to wear. I was sick and you took care of me. I was in prison and you visited me.' Then those who are righteous will reply to him, 'Lord, when did we see you hungry and feed you, or thirsty and give you a drink? When did we see you as a stranger and welcome you, or naked and give you clothes to wear? When did we see you sick or in prison and visit you?' Then the king will reply to them, 'I assure you that when you have done it for one of the least of these brothers and sisters of mine, you have done it for me.'"

WOMEN, WIDOWS, AND THE ELDERLY

1 Timothy 5:2-4 (AMPC): "[Treat] older women like mothers [and] younger women like sisters, in all purity. [Always] treat with great consideration and give aid to those who are truly widowed [solitary and without support]."

IMMEDIATE FAMILY MEMBERS AND RELATIVES (CHILD SUPPORT)

1 Timothy 5:7–9 (NIV): "Give the people these instructions, so that no one may be open to blame. Anyone who does not provide for their relatives, and especially for their own household, has denied the faith and is worse than an unbeliever."

MINISTERS, PASTORS, OR TEACHERS

Galatians 6:6 (NIV): "Nevertheless, the one who receives instruction in the word should share all good things with their instructor."

FELLOW BELIEVERS AND STRANGERS IN NEED

Galatians 6:9–10 (NIV): "Let us not become weary in doing good, for at the proper time we will reap a harvest if we do not give up. Therefore, as we have the opportunity, let us do good to all people, especially to those who belong to the family of believers."

CHAPTER 15

LIVE A WEALTHY LIFE

"We are what we repeatedly do. Excellence, then, is not an act, but a habit."
—Will Durant, paraphrasing Aristotle[74]

When we start out in life, we all aspire to excel generally as human beings. It's natural. Everything about us is designed to move forward, create, and achieve. Even your physical makeup, face, hands, and feet, all point frontwards, not backwards. While personal excellence is admirable and should be pursued, it should not be your life's main goal. As believers and divine spirits, we are actually created for pleasing God in how we live. This is ***true excellence***. After all, the God that created the universe lives and dwells inside of you! Our mindsets should always be positioned with the attitude that we are pleased with what pleases God. Whatever He wants you to do, do it with excellence.

Excellence is not perfection. Instead, it's about delivering at a high standard. To achieve excellence in anything, you must first develop an attitude for wanting to be mature. Maturity is reaching for a final state. For context, we

---

74   Will Durant, *The Story of Philosophy* (New York, NY: Pocket Books, 1991).

all know our final state of existence on this earth is to be transferred into our higher state in spirit, soul, and our new immortal bodies after this old body decays and goes away. However, in the interim, we are renewing our minds to the mind of Jesus because our spirits have already been renewed. We are *currently* reaching for where we are headed as if we are already there! In other words, we should be striving to live heavenly while abiding in this earthly existence. Excellence or maturity in understanding and operating through our divine self is what we are striving for. In doing so, we please God. In obedience to God, excellence will determine how far we go in life.

Is it possible to *see* excellence? Of course! Excellence *is* something that can be seen, and when you see it, it's something to be desired, because excellence is also attractive. The law of attraction is directly connected to efforts and abilities that are done in excellence—mainly because it's rare, and rarity stands out! We should all strive for excellence in everything we do because when it's seen by others, they will want what you possess or at the very least want to be around what you have, simply because what you have stands out and is OUTSTANDING!

Excellence is like putting on royal apparel or putting on God! It's attractive! This is what draws people and favor towards you because of its influence and appeal. Depending on who it may be, it will compel some to want to be good to you or just be around you. For others, it may cause jealousy or envy by no fault of your own. You're simply being your divine self. Excellence will anger those who are against you because they will instinctively know that there is something you have that they lack. And because they won't quite figure out what it is on the surface, they discount you as someone who "thinks" you are better than them. But what they are really grappling with is how they can get what you've got. Like a fine treasure, envious people and the forces of darkness know you possess something valuable. The question is, do you know what you possess?

God has put greatness inside of each one of us. It's our super nature. It's not a fluke or an accident that we all aspire for something greater in life. Whether it's greater relationships, greater careers, greater influence, or greater moves of God for humanity. it's natural to aspire to achieve something above average and far beyond. Average is neither high nor low, rich nor poor, it's just in between.

But **aspiration** is not achievement. Desire alone does not attract the opportunities and people needed for you to grab hold of your divine inheritance and reach your destiny. Excellence is a process, and it requires time and discipline! It's up to you to want to build disciplines you have been given by whatever circumstances you find yourself in already in order to grow. Growth and development are not always fun, nor are they comfortable. But God knows what you will need in advance for where you are going in your life. What you have *right now* **and where you are** *right now* will determine what you are entrusted with tomorrow and long into the future. To gauge your level of maturity, the following are some questions you should ask yourself to determine if you qualify for more of what God has for you.

ARE YOU DISCIPLINED?

Jesus called his 12 followers his disciples. The word "disciple" comes from the word discipline. Even though these men walked with Jesus and heard what He taught them and others around them, they still had to be disciplined in the things of God. Sometimes, discipline requires enduring the same thing over and over until you overcome it before you are released to move on to something greater. Can you complete a task, even if it's boring? These are usually times of strengthening and character building, which are needed to build you up for greater things ahead. But most people simply quit, give in to temptation, or simply remove themselves from these circumstances before they reap the harvest that was in store for them. If God has instructed you to be somewhere, it is imperative that you stay there until He moves you. You may say, "But it's soooo hard!" Exactly, it's meant to be hard because God is developing your trust in him. If you are not fully engaged in the development process of renewing your mind to your higher self, which requires spending time with God and in His word consistently, you won't have the inner strength to continue to possess and maintain the huge life He has planned for you.

I don't know if you exercise on a regular basis, but if you do or if you once did, you probably remember what it was like when you missed a few days or decided to slack off for a while with the intentions of picking it back up sometime later in the future. While exercising regularly, your body was getting accustomed to the intensity of the training, and it would adapt or level off, which means the routine you started with had gotten easier. When that happens, you add more intensity to your regimen. Perhaps it's adding more weight or more reps or both. The idea is to keep your body progressing. As it progresses with more intensity, you begin to see a physical transformation. If you stop or slack off in between for extended periods of time, it feels harder to get back to the same strength levels you were on before you took the break than if you hadn't taken one at all. So is it with training your mind to walk in tune with your spirit. You must train it continually and at different levels.

By reading God's word daily, not only are you training your mind but you are also feeding your spirit divine food. If not, then just like neglecting physical food, it becomes so much harder to do the will of God because you are spiritually malnourished. We know that God is a giver, and He does not give you something then take it away based on your performance. Yet, so many believers lose some of the things that God has already given them because they are blinded by dark tactics used against them and fail to see the value of what they already possess. That's simply a matter of lacking discipline in recognizing, appreciating, and valuing the things of God. God is always moving, directing, and shifting circumstances, events, and people to get you to your divine destiny. Partner with Him by accepting discipline. It's for your good.

> Jeremiah 29: 11–13 (NIV): "For I know the plans I have for you," declares the Lord, "plans to prosper you and not to harm you, plans to give you hope and a future. Then you will call on me and come and pray to me, and I will listen to you. You will seek me and find me when you seek me with all your heart."

ARE YOU OBEDIENT?

Do you move or act on things when God says it's time to do so, or do you move when you want to move? Do you stay in something because of your word, or do you stay because it's easy or for the pay or convenience? To be great in God requires obedience: hearing and acting on what He says and also when He says to do so, like following the cloud where it leads you, as the Israelites did when they were walking in the desert with God. When it moved, they moved.

We've all left careers or relationships because of pressure. It's natural. When something seems too hard or it doesn't look like its working for us, we look for something or someone else. But all pressure is not bad for you. Some pressures are designed to burn off the immaturities of your carnal way of thinking and behavior. We've all experienced some of the greatest and most extraordinary talents and inventions from people who withstood pressure and stayed obedient to what they started. Imagine not having the phone or the airplane today. These modern conveniences exist today because they were invented by people who stuck with their convictions despite scrutiny or pressure from opposing viewpoints. Listen, if God led you to it, then He will strengthen you through it. Trust Him and not your own impulses to quit.

> Romans 5:3–5 (CEB): "We even take pride in our problems, because we know that trouble produces endurance, endurance produces character, and character produces hope. This hope doesn't put us to shame, because the love of God has been poured out in our hearts through the Holy Spirit, who has been given to us."

ARE YOU TRUSTWORTHY?

Can you be trusted? Are you someone who can be depended on, even if you know the result may not fall in your favor? Most people may answer yes to this question. But if you put them to the test, sadly, they'll fall short. It doesn't have to be something big. It can be something as simple as paying someone money you owe them. After all, you were glad they were generous enough to loan it to you when you asked in the beginning. By the way, this is the number one reason why I don't loan money to someone; I'll give it instead. This way, the person is released and free from any financial obligation towards me.

Or maybe you have trouble simply being on time or punctual. What is your attitude when *you* have to wait for someone? For example, if a store wasn't open at 9:45 a.m. when it's clearly posted on the door that it opens at 9 a.m. Or your favorite television program or movie didn't show when the program guide said it would? Or what if the pastor of your church was consistently late? How would you feel about any of those scenarios? Being consistently late and causing someone to wait for you is showing disrespect for the other person's time. And it's worse when the tardiness becomes your reputation. If an advance or promotion opportunity existed on your job that required punctuality, you'd simply get overlooked because you can't be trusted with time.

And time is an ingredient of money. I worked with a personal trainer who was consistently late when we had training sessions. When he wanted to extend our agreement for more sessions, I declined. Unfortunately, many other clients refused to extend their contracts, as this had become his reputation. He still gets new clients, but few stick with him because of his lack of punctuality. Because of this, his business has not grown but instead has remained at the same mediocre levels year after year.

Do you have to get paid in order to perform at your best? Or if the task is not something you enjoy, do you work it to perfection regardless? It doesn't have to all be work related. It can be something as simple as putting things back in their proper places, such as a basket at the grocery store, or cleaning up behind yourself so someone else doesn't have to. Or just simply doing what you said you would do. If you grew a reputation that you cannot be depended upon in the eyes of people, will God override that and trust you with something greater? Sometimes it may have nothing to do with doing as much as it has to do with the attitude with which you do it.

> Luke 16:10–12 (NIV): "Whoever can be trusted with very little can also be trusted with much, and whoever is dishonest with very little will also be dishonest with much. So, if you have not been trustworthy in handling worldly wealth, who will trust you with true riches? And if you have not been trustworthy with someone else's property, who will give you property of your own?"

DO YOU COMPROMISE?

Compromise *will* delay God's best in your life and will simultaneously stunt your growth and ability for maturity. Compromise is not exactly turning away from God, although it is flirting with disobedience. By compromising, you may experience a bit of short-term satisfaction but that should never be your goal. Continual small delays tied together will lead to you eventually running out of time, and the result could be a wasted and unfulfilled life. In my opinion, it's sad when I see an older adult who has yet to make good decisions in the areas of their life that requires them to be more patient, loving, giving, or disciplined. It's sad because I would bet that they've had multiple opportunities to do so. However, in fairness, everyone matures at a different moment in time, which is why we have until death to try and get some things right.

How do you compromise? When people can't distinguish the difference between you who professes to live by the standards of God and someone who does not, then clearly there should be something about the way you are living before others you should give attention to in addressing. We know we have freedom in the divine, but our freedom should not be exercised at the expense of confusing others who live life guided by their lower selves. The higher self should not give in to the lower self as others do—if they get drunk, you get drunk; they curse, so you curse; they lie and cheat, then you lie and cheat. If you do, then don't be surprised that when they get sick, you get sick, they get laid off, and you get laid off, they lose money, and you lose money, they have troubled relationships, you have troubled relationships. Instead, be the standard for excellence and the kingdom of the light. Remember, it's rare but it's attractive.

Keep in mind that the goal of the forces of darkness is to keep you from experiencing the power and truth of the God inside you. This is done by keeping you spiritually ignorant and occupied by operating through the senses and not the spirit. To be carnal is his goal for you. Carnality has limited power. He will try and make you pay every time you don't compromise to eventually get you to the place where you begin to wonder if this "divine walk with God" thing is even worth it. Believe me, it most definitely is! Don't compromise in the eyes of people and don't compromise on the word of God. As believers we must have standards, and those standards should be balanced against God's word. Without standards, then every man will do what seems right in his own eyes.

Proverbs 12:15 (NIV): "The way of fools seems right to them, but the wise listen to advice."

CAN YOU ENDURE?

Giving up or giving in too soon is the biggest mistake a believer can make. Excellence is not about how high in God you can go, but how low in God you are willing to humble yourself. The lower you go in Him, the higher He will lift you! The things that you desire is not all that God is trying to give you. He wants to also mature you so that when "the things" come, you have them, but they don't have you, never losing sight that He is all you really need. And with Him comes *everything*!

2 Corinthians 6:3–10 (CEB): "We don't give anyone any reason to be offended about anything so that our ministry won't be criticized. Instead, we commend ourselves as ministers of God in every way. We did this with our great endurance through problems, disasters, and stressful situations. We went through beatings, imprisonments, and riots. We experienced hard work, sleepless nights, and hunger. We displayed purity, knowledge, patience, and generosity. We served with the Holy Spirit, genuine love, telling the truth, and God's power. We carried the weapons of righteousness in our right hand and our left hand. We were treated with honor and dishonor and with verbal abuse and good evaluation. We were seen as both fake and real, as unknown and well known, as dying—and look, we are alive! We were seen as punished but not killed, as going through pain but always happy, as poor but making many rich, and as having nothing but owning everything."

LOVE

When I began this book, one of the first subjects I addressed was that God is good and everything about Him is good. It's all good. In fact, you can't say or spell the word good without God in it. As I continued, we discovered that not only is He good, but that He is Spirit; therefore, we are spirit. God is light; therefore, we are children of light and not darkness. Everything that God is we are also. And perhaps you were even surprised to read that we are gods.

If God is a noun, then what He does is the adjective. But what He **does**, does not describe what He is. Instead, what He is describes what He does. We know that God loves, but the Bible says that God **is** Love.

1 John 4:7–8 (NIV): "Dear friends, let us love one another, for love comes from God. Everyone who loves has been born of God and knows God. Whoever does not love does not know God, because God is love."

Love is the most talked about, sung about, written about, and discussed topic in the entire world. It's been expressed in so many different forms, yet has not been truly defined as to what love is. Only the Bible dares to define and declare what love actually is, and it says that "God is love." If that is what He is, then as His children that's what we are also. We are love and not hate. Love is the very essence of not who He is, but what He is. In fact, love not only comes *from* Him, but it is clearly *of* Him. Love is the DNA of God! And you are the purest expression and result of love. If you have children, then you know that they are the direct result of two people in the act of love. If you can define God, then you can define love.

Often, people define love as a feeling or an emotion. Emotions are a conscious mental reaction (anger or fear) subjectively experienced as a strong feeling usually directed toward a specific object and typically accompanied by physiological and behavioral changes in the body, which is why emotions are expressed in terms of "How did that make you feel?" or "It made me feel this way." Emotions are reactions and expressions of something deeper that caused them.

God is not a reactor or a reaction; He is action. Love always acts or responds! Love is always in motion. Love is ever present. And Love is always now. He responds or acts long before we need Him to. So, if we are to define love, then we must try and define God. God cannot be defined, and words cannot describe all of what He is. But words **can** describe His actions.

1 Corinthians 13:1–8 (NIV): "If I speak in the tongues of men or of angels, but do not have love, I am only a resounding gong or a clanging cymbal. If I have the gift of prophecy and can fathom all mysteries and all knowledge, and if I have a faith that can move mountains, but do not have love, I am nothing. If I give all I possess to the poor and give over my body to hardship

that I may boast, but do not have love, I gain nothing. Love is patient, love is kind. It does not envy, it does not boast, it is not proud. It does not dishonor others, it is not self-seeking, it is not easily angered, and it keeps no record of wrongs. Love does not delight in evil but rejoices with the truth. It always protects, always trusts, always hopes, and always perseveres. Love never fails."

If this is how God acts, then this is also how we ought to act. Keep in mind, I understand that acting in love is not something that is **humanly** possible. If acting in love were possible and could be done in human effort, then there would have been no need for redemption. However, acting in love is a choice. And when we choose to act in love or be like God, that's when we experience His power! God's Spirit is like a generator, which produces power that's expressed through joy.

Love is always God's will. It's what He is. And when love is the motivation, you don't need to ask for God's permission. It's always the right choice. When we are not living life from the attitude of walking in love, we are not walking in the power and submission of God, which is by the Holy Spirit. It is the forces of darkness that want you to live and walk in frustration, depression, confusion, anxiousness, fear, jealousy, or downright hatred. These are all signs that you have given in to your flesh and have willingly walked away from your true divine nature. Your spirit is running low on joy and losing power. The devil knows this, so why don't we know this?

Ephesians 5:8–14 (CEB) says: "You were once darkness, but now you are light in the Lord, so live your life as children of light. Light produces fruit that consists of every sort of goodness, justice, and truth. Therefore, test everything to see what's pleasing to the Lord and don't participate in the unfruitful actions of darkness. Instead, you should reveal the truth about them. It's embarrassing to even talk about what certain persons do in secret. But everything exposed to the light is revealed by the light. Everything that is revealed by the light is light."

Therefore, God commands us to do and be one thing. And that is to love. God is not asking us; He is commanding us to love—because love is not what we do or show, it's what we are. Anything that functions apart from its original intent is considered to be dysfunctional. If a car does not start when you activate the starter, then clearly something is wrong with the car, not the manufacturer or the maker of it. So, when something does not seem to work correctly in our lives, why is it that we question the maker and not the function of the one made?

Forgiveness is the fix-all for everything that flows through Heaven. When offenses come, rub some forgiveness on it. Love is the power source of our faith, but forgiveness is the reactivator for love when faith tends to sputter. Without forgiveness, our faith becomes ineffective. This is why the enemy stirs up so much dissention between believers and people in general—because when we are not walking in *love*, then we are not walking in *power*. And until we recognize this, we can never reach our full potential because we are still immature in God and the things of God. Afterall, are you not gods? LOVE is the answer to every problem that you or I could ever face. If love is not the answer, then what is?

PERSONAL TESTIMONIES

Being disciplined, obedient, being found trustworthy and not compromising are critical key elements to your divine walk because God is *always* trying to get something to you, but His desire is to do it through you. The goal is your maturity. He wants you mature in your faith. Why? So that you look like Him. This is what makes us so different from those who live by their lower nature. We are not excused from challenges in this world, but the difference is we don't crumble and fold up when we are faced with issues from darkness and the curse, because we have answers and solutions to problems.

We overcome the schemes and all the power of the enemy through what Jesus has already done for us through his shed blood and by the words that we profess as believers. We should walk through our circumstances with peace and not worry, because we always triumph in our battles. We are children of the kingdom of Heaven, and our mission is to replicate God's kingdom on this earth. Once hope comes, you are on the doorstep of your deliverance or manifestation of what you have desired. How do we know this? Hope shows us that something is possible, and hope is what fuels our faith.

James 1:2–4 (NIV) says, "Consider it pure joy, my brothers and sisters, whenever you face trials of many kinds, because you know that the testing of your faith produces perseverance. Let perseverance finish its work so that you may be mature and complete, not lacking anything."

In this "testing of our faith," we find that it produces the ingredients necessary to develop us so that nothing can defeat us, and nothing is too hard or impossible. When our faith is strong, it brings what is invisible to the visible. When it becomes visible, it becomes real. And once it's real to you, then you have something so powerful that no one can deny it. And that is your testimony.

A testimony is described as something that someone says, especially in a court of law while formally promising to tell the truth, as proof or evidence that something exists or is true.

Your testimony is a documented fact or proof of your belief. It's evidence that the unseen realm is real and documented on earth as your manifested gift and recorded in the books of Heaven, where it was already done. "Thy will be done, on earth as it is in Heaven." Once a testimony has been produced, it becomes the proof by which you will be judged by the enemy and the evidence of that which you plead your case before God.

Revelation 12:10–11 (NIV) says, "Then I heard a loud voice in Heaven say: 'Now have come the salvation and the power and the kingdom of our God, and the authority of his Messiah. For the accuser of our brothers and sisters, who accuses them before our God day and night, has been hurled down. They triumphed over him by the blood of the Lamb and by the word of their TESTIMONY...'"

We can break every power of the enemy that comes against us because we have been purchased by Jesus's blood. And He has given us the power to do so. This is our testimony! But you can't have a testimony without a test. There is nothing in this world that we cannot overcome through the power we have received through our Lord, Jesus. But it requires the pursuit of excellence in knowing His word and walking through it in the power of the Spirit. Your *attitude* in the trials you face determines your *altitude* and your deliverance and how high you go in Christ.

Saint Francis of Assisi said, "Preach the Gospel to everyone and use words if necessary." I think what he was saying is that living the examples of the gospel is more effective than words we say about the gospel. Some people may argue with you about doctrine or interpretation of scripture, but unless they believe you're a liar, they can't argue with your testimony. There is nothing more powerful than a miraculous testimony. Jesus and his disciples used them to confirm that the words that they spoke were truth, bringing Heaven to earth. I know personally that the word of God changes lives, which is why I use my testimonies, because people relate to stories and the things that have actually manifested and made a difference in my life.

Your salvation is a testimony. It's evidence that you have changed and have reconnected to the divine through acceptance of Jesus's sacrificial death. But overcoming circumstances should be your testimony also. It's great when you can point to a miracle that took place in the Bible or maybe even a miracle you've heard that's happened to someone else in another state or another country, but how impactful is God's word when you or someone you know experiences a miracle for themselves? It doesn't just change your life, but it's also designed to help change the lives of those around you. Knowing that what God did for you, He will do for me and anyone who has faith and truly believes in what He said.

CONCLUSION

In the first chapter, I discussed the film *The Lion King* and how it's natural to aspire to share everything you've learned and acquired throughout your life with your descendants. While the film began in this manner, it was not the entire story. You see, Simba fled the kingdom following his father's death out of fear and condemnation, because he believed the lie that his disobedience was the cause of his death. It was his evil Uncle Scar who duped him, because he believed he was the legitimate heir to the throne. Unfortunately, this deceptive story and devilish scheme succeeded in convincing Simba to abandon the land that was legally his and seek refuge in the jungle. He was later befriended by a warthog and a meerkat, who taught him to live without rules or ambition and simply lay around eating bugs all day, rather than hunt and rule as he was created to do. To Simba, this appeared to be a reasonable and plausible philosophy. "Hakuna-matata" became their new life motto, which translates as "no trouble" or "no worries" and "relax." This was probably acceptable for a warthog or a meerkat, but not for a lion born to rule, particularly now that the kingdom he has abandoned has begun to deteriorate due to drought, poverty, lack, sickness, and a wicked ruler who couldn't care less about the lion pride. This story parallels our lives in numerous ways. You see, if you've been born again, you now possess God's mighty spirit, just as Simba possessed Mufasa's spirit. However, because we believe the enemy's lies, we believe there is nothing we can do about deception, darkness, sickness, disease, poverty, and lack in our own lives, let alone the lives of others. If you are a believer, then *you* are the answer to the world's problems. However, you cannot solve the world's problems until you have stepped out in faith, trusted God with your own problems, and applied His word to yourself.

ARE YOU A BABOON?

The good news about ***The Lion King's*** remaining chapters is that Simba finally comes to terms with who he is and what he was born to become. Regrettably, it took a baboon to point this out to him and bring it to his attention. This was a watershed moment because the baboon referred to the lion as a baboon. During this exchange, Simba responded by saying, "I think someone is confused." I love what the baboon, named Rafiki, says in response to that. He tells him that he wasn't the one who was perplexed; instead, you are! Because you do not know who you are! He pointedly told him, "You are Mufasa's son!"[75] In other words, because you are the son of a dead king, you are also now a king. Simba eventually realized who he was and confronted his evil uncle and the lies he concocted to deceive him. They fought, but Simba won.

Regrettably, believers all over the world live this way. That is, they are unaware of who they truly are, what they truly possess, or how to obtain it. Then consider me to be the baboon pointing this scenario out to you. You are royal, possess a kingdom, and can possess anything the light touches. All that is required of you is to trust the God within and follow His guidance. You will have to fight for what you want but take heart: God has already defeated the adversary who is attempting to deprive you of what is rightfully yours. The way to profit in life is to put your complete trust in Jesus's completed work, to be bold enough to desire great things for yourself, and to believe they are rightfully yours—just as Simba did.

---

75   *The Lion King.*

ACKNOWLEDGMENTS

Thank you, Jesus, my King. For loving me more than I could ever know to love myself. For not letting me go when I so desperately wanted to give up. And never condemning me when I so felt I deserved to be. For protecting me through thousands of miles of traveling. For granting me a family to love and be loved. And for sacrificing your life so that I can have an abundant life. With this book and this life I have, I give it back to you. Do with it what you will. You know what's best for me.

To my many pastors and teachers who walked me through God's word, Dr. Ed Montgomery and Dr. Scott Davenport - Houston, TX, Pastor Mark Filkey - Stockton, CA, Greg Tyler, chaplain of the Houston Texans football team, Dr. Phillip Goudeaux - Sacramento, CA, and my current pastors for life, Joel and Victoria Osteen - Houston, TX. Thank you for saying yes to God's call. The lives you've changed and will continue to change are countless. Thank you personally for shaping who I am today.

To all my spiritual brothers and sisters, and there are many, thank you for the wisdom and countless hours you poured into me. As I humbled myself at your feet, you all showed me what character, integrity, and a "man of God" looks, acts, and sounds like. You taught me that it's ok to be myself and encouraged me in very tough and difficult times. You loved me enough to tell me the hard things I needed to hear. You sat with me in dark times and cele-brated with me in victories. Today, I am a culmination of all your friendships and brotherhood of which I could never repay.

To my disciples, thank you for trusting my guidance and tutelage. Many times you could have questioned my motives or second-guessed my advice. Instead, you inspected my life, called me when you could have called any-one else in the world, and accepted what I had to say as if it was from God himself. That takes trust and courage. Because of this, I and my family have benefited in ways you cannot imagine.

And to my loving wife, Wanda. The Bible says when a man finds a wife, he's found a good thing. You are my good thing. Because of you, I pursued God more intentionally. Because of you, I learned to embrace who I am. Because of you, I discovered and experienced real love. It was you who told me I had so many gifts and talents inside of me. Because I was so lost, it was you that taught me to look inside to find what I needed. Because of you I dream and believe all things are possible. You permit me to pursue. You keep life inter-esting and you've taught me to dig deeper. In tough times, you helped hold things together and reminded me I was not alone. You're gorgeous and your true beauty is your strength and willingness to do what's hard. Your charac-ter is your courage and your love for me is my reward for being here on this earth. Your smile and laughter alone make my life worth living. Thank you for all I aspire to become.

CPSIA information can be obtained
at www.ICGtesting.com
Printed in the USA
LVHW081631230222
711840LV00003B/91